The Exchange Student Guidebook

The Exchange Student Guidebook

Everything You'll Need to Spend a Successful High School Year Abroad

Olav Schewe

iUniverse, Inc.
Bloomington

The Exchange Student Guidebook
Everything You'll Need to Spend a Successful High School Year Abroad

This book is based on another book, Utvekslingselev, written by the same author and first published by Fagbokforlaget in 2010.

The information provided in this book is designed to provide helpful information and represents the author's expressed opinions, not those of any related parties or entities. All individuals are unique, as are the situations and experiences they encounter. The advice offered in this book is of a general nature and may not be suitable for your situation. Neither the author nor the publisher shall be held liable or responsible with respect to any loss or incidental or consequential damages caused, or alleged to have been caused, directly or indirectly, by the information or advice provided in this book.

iUniverse books may be ordered through booksellers or by contacting:

iUniverse
1663 Liberty Drive
Bloomington, IN 47403
www.iuniverse.com
1-800-Authors (1-800-288-4677)

Because of the dynamic nature of the Internet, any web addresses or links contained in this book may have changed since publication and may no longer be valid. The views expressed in this work are solely those of the author and do not necessarily reflect the views of the publisher, and the publisher hereby disclaims any responsibility for them.

Cover design: Jacob Holmberg
Author photograph: Hilde Karine Sæberg
Cover photograph: © iStockphoto
Illustrations: Lars Petter Hermansen and Ola Olsen Lysgaard

ISBN: 978-1-4759-5159-2 (sc)
ISBN: 978-1-4759-5161-5 (hc)
ISBN: 978-1-4759-5160-8 (ebk)

Printed in the United States of America

iUniverse rev. date: 11/20/2012

To my parents and host parents,
Elisabeth, Theo, David, and Marybeth, for their support and
belief in me.

www.exchangestudentbook.com

Contents

Preface

In 1947, the first high school exchange students left their homes to go to school and live with families abroad. Since then, the term *exchange student* has gone from covering only just a handful of people to now including tens of thousands of young students each year.

There are several reasons it has become so popular to spend a school year abroad. As an exchange student, you get the chance to go out into the world and see it through your own eyes. By living with a host family and going to a secondary school, you will become part of the local community. This will help you learn the language and experience a new culture "from the inside out." It is this last benefit, above all else, that makes a high school year abroad something unique!

Spending a school year abroad is not only a great experience. It is also an investment in yourself and your future. International experience, language skills, and knowledge of foreign cultures are more important now than ever, and a school year abroad gives you all three.

It is important to remember, however, that an exchange year is not one long holiday. In fact, it can be pretty tough sometimes. It may take time to adjust to the new culture and to find new friends. It is therefore important to be motivated and to have realistic expectations before deciding to begin on this adventure.

Whether you have already decided to go on an exchange or are still considering it, you will probably have many questions. This book aims to answer those questions and to show you what an exchange year is really about. It is a book that will make you more secure about what is awaiting you. The goal is to prepare you for life as an exchange student and help you deal with all the practical issues that come with spending a school year abroad. But perhaps most important, this book will give you advice on the many new situations you will encounter and help you tackle common challenges. The purpose of all of this is to provide you with a foundation for a successful and memorable year. Good luck!

How to Read This Book

This book is divided into twenty-eight chapters and four major parts for readability and easy reference. You may read this book from start to finish or just read the sections most interesting to you, and you can start reading at any time before or during your exchange experience. However, to get the most out of it, we recommend that you read parts 2 and 3 (and part 4, if you are going to the USA) well ahead of your departure time.

This book does not recommend any one host country over another. Parts 1, 2, and 3 apply to all exchange students, regardless of destination country. But because so many students choose to go to the USA, we have included part 4, which has specific information for those students.

Part 1: About Student Exchange

Part 1 contains basic information intended for anyone who wants to learn more about student exchange. Students who have not yet decided whether to sign up for an exchange program will find this part particularly useful.

Part 2: Pre-Departure

Part 2 contains information and advice relevant for the period starting when someone decides to become an exchange student until the departure.

Part 3: Abroad

Part 3 contains information and advice relevant for the period from the first day in the host country until the return home.

Part 4: Exchange to the USA

Part 4 contains information specifically for students going to the USA or students who are interested in going there. Note that in this part, the terms *America* and *Americans* refer to the United States of America (USA) and its citizens. The use of these terms is for practical reasons and is not intended to offend anyone from other parts of the Americas.

History

During the worst fighting of World Wars I and II, a volunteer group from the USA known as the American Field Service was working in Europe transporting injured Allied soldiers. Through their work, the members learned that personal contact with people from foreign nations contributed to mutual understanding and friendship.

When the members of the group returned to the United States after the wars were over, they wanted to use what they had learned to create more understanding and friendship across borders. Their goal was peace among nations: they decided that the world should never again have to suffer what it had experienced over the previous forty years.

In 1947, these people started an exchange program, inviting foreign students to live in the USA for one year. The idea was that the foreign students would go to school in the USA and learn about American culture, and in the process, Americans would learn about the culture of the visiting students.

Since then, the number of exchange students has risen yearly. Across the world today, it is estimated that from fifty thousand to one hundred thousand high school students participate in exchange programs every year.

Much has changed since 1947. The number of countries exchange students can travel to has increased dramatically, and so has the number of student exchange organizations. Meanwhile, technology has made it easier than ever to be an exchange student. However, the original idea behind student exchange remains the same: personal contact across cultures contributes to global peace and understanding.

PART
1

ABOUT STUDENT EXCHANGE

Chapter 1

Introduction: The Basics

You're young, you're curious, and you feel that the world awaits you. You want to experience something new and different, and you want to do it now. Maybe you want to get a taste of American hospitality and high school spirit. Or maybe you want to see what it's like to live in the Far East. Perhaps you don't yet know what you want—and that's okay, too. As long as you are young, curious, and want to experience another culture and learn a new language, the world of student exchange is probably right for you!

What Is a High School Exchange Student?

A high school exchange student is someone eighteen years old or younger who travels to a foreign country to live there and attend a local high school. In some cases, the student can live at the school (boarding school). However, it is far more common for exchange students to stay with a family, commonly referred to as a *host family*.

Fun fact—Did you know that . . .
Germany sends more exchange students abroad than any other country? More than twenty thousand young people leave Germany every year to go to high school in a different country.

How Can I Become an Exchange Student?

If you already know a family in another country where you would like to live, you can theoretically organize an exchange year solely on your own. However, it should be noted that with some countries, such as the USA, organizing an exchange yourself is very difficult due to visa regulations. In any case, you would need to arrange a visa, enroll at a school, and take charge of all the logistics yourself.

It is therefore much more common to use an organization—such as AFS, EF, Rotary, YFU, and others—that specializes in student exchange programs. There are many advantages of using an exchange organization. First, the organization takes care of practical matters such as finding a host family, enrolling you in a high school, providing you with the necessary visa documents, and booking your flights. Second, the exchange organization helps prepare you for the coming year and usually gives you the opportunity to meet other students who are also going on exchange. Finally, the organization provides support before and during the exchange year. They will answer questions and assist you if you encounter difficulties while abroad.

How Long Does an Exchange Program Last?

There are programs of varying lengths. Half-year programs are gaining popularity, but the traditional one-year programs are by far the most common.

Where Can I Go?

Most exchange organizations let students choose from a range of host countries in all parts of the world.

Requirements—Who Can Become an Exchange Student?

The requirements for going on exchange depend on the rules of the host country and the exchange organization. There are slight variations, but the following requirements seem common to most organizations:

- You have to be between fourteen and eighteen years old on the day of travel.
- You have to have been a full-time student prior to departure.
- You have to have reasonably good grades in school.
- You have to be in good mental and physical health.
- You have to be motivated and open to change.

Fun fact—Did you know that ...
many exchange students begin to dream in their host country's language after only a couple of weeks?

How Will the Exchange Year Fit with My High School Education?

In some countries like the USA and Mexico, where students typically finish high school at age seventeen or eighteen, students can go on exchange after graduating from high school and use the exchange experience as an "in-between year" (gap year) before continuing their formal education or entering the work force. This is also common practice in Belgium, although students there finish high school at age eighteen or nineteen. In most countries, however, students go on exchange while still in high school at home. The students can then either incorporate the year abroad as one year of high school at home or spend it as an extra year of high school. Practices vary from country to country, and sometimes from school to school.

Other Options for Exchange

Some high schools have their own exchange programs or agreements with schools abroad. These programs are often shorter than a full year and can be quite different from a traditional school year abroad. Talk to your school counselor to find out if your school has this type of program.

Useful Terms

Jet Lag

Jet lag is a condition that occurs when flying east or west to another time zone, causing your sleep pattern or day and night rhythms to get out of balance. The symptoms may include tiredness, difficulty sleeping, and irritability. Jet lag is harmless and will go away on its own within one to ten days.

Contact Person/Coordinator

As an exchange student, you will have a person in the host country to assist and support you throughout the year. This person is the exchange organization's local representative and is usually responsible for several students in a given geographical area. Often these coordinators work as volunteers (that is, without pay).

Culture Shock

Anyone who travels to a foreign country can experience culture shock. The new culture may seem confusing and strange, making it difficult for the visitor to know how to relate to others. Culture shock usually occurs at the beginning of the stay, and it rarely lasts long.

Exchange Student

That is you!

Exchange Organization

This is the organization that arranges the student exchange. This organization in your home country cooperates with another branch of its own organization or a partner organization in the host country. That organization, in turn, will provide you with a host family and contact person in the country where you will be living.

Host Family

The family you live with in the host country is your host family. It consists of host parents and perhaps host sisters and host brothers.

Host Country

This is the country where you live as an exchange student.

Reverse Culture Shock

Reverse culture shock can occur when an exchange student returns to his or her home country. Because the student has adapted to the host culture, now it's the home culture that seems confusing and strange. This feeling may or may not be stronger than the initial culture shock.

Visa

This is sort of like an entry permit to a foreign country. Most countries require a visa for exchange students. Usually you apply for a visa by contacting the host country's embassy in your home country prior to leaving to study abroad.

Chapter 2

Reasons for Going

There are many good reasons for spending a school year abroad. Here are some of them:

You will have fun and experience a lot.
It is no wonder that many former exchange students look back on their year abroad as the best year of their lives. Exchange students have many new and exciting experiences, and they usually have a lot of fun.

You will learn a language.
As an exchange student, you get free language training all day long! You will speak your new language at school, with your host family, with your new friends, and at the store. You'll hear it on the radio and television. In other words, you'll be learning all the time! You will also learn to read and write your new language in school. How good you eventually become will depend on the effort you put into learning, but everything is set up for you to become fluent in a foreign language.

You will learn a new culture—from the inside out!
As an exchange student, you will not need to read a stack of books to become an expert in your host country and its culture. You're already there, experiencing everything yourself—not as a tourist, but as a family member, as a student, and as part

of a group of friends. In other words, you'll learn about your host country from the inside out!

You will get to know yourself better.

As an exchange student, you will have the opportunity to see yourself from a whole new perspective. By the end of your time abroad, you will be more secure about who you are, what you like, and what you stand for.

You will get to know your own culture better.

Just as you will see and experience a new culture from the inside out, you also will see your own culture from the outside. Because you will be confronted by cultural differences on a daily basis, you will learn not only about your host country's culture, but also about your own.

You will make new friends.

Meeting new people is one of the greatest advantages of being an exchange student. You are likely to make strong new friendships, some of which may last a lifetime.

You will pick up valuable knowledge and skills that can help your career.

In today's globalized world, international experience and good language skills are becoming increasingly important. What you learn abroad can be a great asset as you establish your professional career.

You will become more independent and mature.

During your year abroad, you will face many new situations and also a number of challenges. When you do not have your parents nearby, you'll get better at looking after yourself and resolving your own difficulties.

You will promote peace and understanding.
Contact across cultures promotes peace and understanding. This was the original idea behind student exchange, and it is perhaps more important now than ever.

It's the chance of a lifetime.
You can visit a foreign country at any time in your life. However, to live in a country as a high school exchange student, experiencing the culture this deeply and closely, is a chance you'll get only once.

It doesn't have to be expensive.
Since you will live and eat with your host family, life as an exchange student does not have to be more expensive than living at home. In fact, depending on where you go, it can actually be cheaper. And compared to many other educational programs abroad, high school exchange is often relatively inexpensive. Another thing to keep in mind is that you can often apply for a variety of scholarships to finance the experience.

It has proven benefits.
Many of the advantages associated with spending a year abroad have been scientifically proven. In a 2005 study conducted by Dr. Mitchell Hammer, exchange students were found to have gained the following benefits:

- greater intercultural competence
- greater knowledge of the host culture
- greater fluency in the language of the host country
- less anxiety when interacting with people from different countries
- more friendships with people from other cultures
- broader intercultural networks

Real-life experience

My exchange year in New Zealand was a fantastic year I'll never forget, a year filled with exciting adventures and top friends that I will never lose touch with. There were ups and downs, of course, but I think that contributed to strengthening me as a person. You *grow* a lot during an exchange year!

—former exchange student to New Zealand

Chapter 3
What Are the Costs?

The total price for your entire experience will depend on which country you visit, how much you spend there (pocket money plus travel expenses), which exchange organization you use, and whether you receive any scholarships. Since you will be living and eating with your host family, the relevant expenses can be divided into four categories:

- a program fee or participation fee (paid to the exchange organization)
- necessary expenses not covered by the program fee
- pocket money in the host country
- travels and day trips in the host country

The Program Fee

The program fee or participation fee is what the exchange organization charges for arranging your year. The fee covers placement with a host family, school registration, pretravel materials, visa assistance, and guidance during your stay abroad. Usually the travel cost (flight tickets) will be included, as well. The fee may include more help and services, depending on the organization, so the size of the fee will vary accordingly. Therefore, when comparing exchange organizations, it is important to look at what's included in the fee itself. To make this process easier, we have provided a list of common expenses related to an exchange year.

Prior to Departure	Abroad
• application fee (interview fee) • travel insurance • cancellation insurance • visa fees • medical examination • immunization/vaccines • domestic transportation from your home to an international airport • travel to/from the host country • a gift for your host family	• preparation/orientation camp (possibly) • language class (possibly) • school books and materials • school uniform (possibly) • daily school transportation • sports and leisure activities • lunch bought at school

Fun fact—Did you know that . . .
the names for the currencies used in Sweden (*krona*), Norway (*krone*), and the Czech Republic (*koruna*) all mean "crown"?

Pocket Money

How much spending money you will need depends on your spending habits and which country you are going to. Some countries are cheaper than others; for example, you would need less pocket money in a country like Costa Rica than you would in France.

What should the pocket money cover?

As a rule of thumb, plan to use your own money for all activities conducted apart from your host family (cinema, fast food, leisure activities, sports, dance classes, bus tickets, clothes, shopping, etc.).

How much pocket money do I need to bring?

It is possible to live economically abroad. However, living on a small budget can have its disadvantages. Having to say no when your new friends ask you to join them for bowling or some other activity that costs money could hinder your social life. Ask the exchange organization what monthly amount they recommend for your host country, or talk with former exchange students.

Traveling in the Host Country

As an exchange student, you will probably get the opportunity do some traveling while in the host country. You might travel with your host family, your school, your exchange organization, or your sports team. In some cases, you may be able to do some traveling on your own or with friends. When traveling without your host family, you should always be prepared to pay all the costs yourself. If you travel with your host family, payment arrangements can vary depending on the type of travel, your host family, and what is common in the host country.

Of course, you can save money by choosing not to travel while you're in the host country. Be aware, though, that you might miss a unique opportunity to see even more of your new country at a low cost. Local people often have access to cheap ways of traveling, and your biggest travel expense—the flight from your home country to your host country—has already been covered. That being said, if you don't get the opportunity to travel as much as you had hoped, don't let it bother you. Travel is not the main goal of an exchange year anyway, so if you do get the chance, consider it a bonus to the rest of the year.

> **Travel advice**
> Do not go on exchange with too little money, and be realistic about how much you will spend. If you can, save up some money or get a summer job before you go. By doing this, even if you choose not to spend much money, you won't have to worry about missing out on anything.

Scholarships and Financial Aid

In some countries, the government offers scholarships to exchange students. Some exchange organizations also offer scholarships for students. Ask your exchange organization about scholarships and financial support. Note that deadlines for applying for scholarships may vary.

> **Travel advice**
> Find out as early as possible if there are any scholarships you can apply for.

Can I work and earn money while abroad?

As an exchange student, you are in the host country to go to school and to experience a new culture—not to work. If you are staying on a student visa, you may even be violating some laws or regulations if you accept paid work. In the USA, for example, taking unauthorized employment is strictly forbidden and may result in you being sent back to your home country.

Sometimes, however, exchange students are offered the chance to earn some pocket money by doing chores, like babysitting or yard work for a neighbor, and this is usually okay. Other jobs, like co-coaching a sports team or tutoring after school, may also be okay, but check to make sure beforehand. Whatever you choose to do, never become dependent on having to earn money while staying abroad.

Chapter 4

Is an Exchange Year Right for Me?

A year away from family, friends, and all that is familiar impacts students in different ways. For some students, a little homesickness now and then is not a serious problem. For others, however, it may be a bigger challenge. In fact, it can sometimes be pretty tough to be an exchange student, so it is important to be motivated if you decide to spend a school year abroad.

Most exchange students report that their year abroad was the experience of a lifetime—often the greatest year of their lives. But there are also exchange students who decide to leave the program and go home early. Some of the reasons for this could be expectations that were too high, poor motivation, inability to adapt to a new lifestyle, homesickness, or problems with the host family.

For many, whether or not to become an exchange student is a major decision. In order to make a good decision, it is important that you know what you can reasonably expect from the experience.

Be realistic!

A common characteristic among disappointed exchange students is that they have sky-high expectations before the year begins. You cannot expect your host family to have a large, luxurious house and a swimming pool. And you cannot expect to attend a school where you do not need to do any homework, or where you will make a lot of friends on the first day. The fact is that most host families are quite normal families with average incomes. Most schools require effort from their students, and it may take some time to make new friends. Remember that a school year abroad is not a yearlong holiday: it is a year as a student in a foreign country. If you have unrealistic expectations, you will be easily disappointed. Besides, it is not the size of your host family's house that will determine whether or not you enjoy the experience!

So what can you expect? You can expect to live in a new and exciting place—a place where you will see, learn, and experience more than could fill a hundred books. You can expect to come to a family that is looking forward to getting to know you better. This family will be interested in learning about you, your way of life, and your culture. You can also expect to come to a new and exciting school where you'll learn things you wouldn't have learned at your own school at home.

Common Challenges

When you consider going abroad, it is important to remember that, just like at home, no two days are alike. Most days are good, some days are absolutely fantastic, and other days can be difficult. You will have plenty of exciting experiences, but you also will encounter challenges. Here are some examples:

Homesickness

It is common to experience homesickness from time to time when living abroad. Whether the homesickness becomes troublesome or not depends on how you handle it. In chapter 17, you'll find more information on homesickness, how to deal with it, and how to prevent it.

School

You may find that you have to spend more time on homework than you're used to, and that your new school generally expects more of you than your school at home did.

Making new friends

It may take some time to make new friends. Often you'll need to be the one who takes the initiative or starts the conversation.

Feeling tired

As an exchange student, life is usually fast-paced, and you will have a lot to get used to. You must adapt to a new climate, new food, a new family, and a new school—all while speaking a different language. Therefore, it is not surprising that exchange students often feel tired!

Host family

It is difficult to know in advance what kind of host family you will get. Having to adapt to a new family can be challenging. You might need to help around the house more than you are used to, and the family's rules may be very different from those of your family at home. Remember, you are the one who has to adapt to the host family—not the other way around.

Having said all of this, challenges make exchange students grow and develop. Those who face more challenges than others probably grow the most as individuals during their exchange year.

Will I Enjoy Being an Exchange Student?

It is difficult to know exactly what your school year abroad will be like. And it is even more difficult to know how you will deal with all the new situations you will face as an exchange student. Therefore, it is not possible to guarantee that you will enjoy the experience or that it will be exactly as you imagine.

The most important personal qualities for achieving a successful year are motivation and openness to new experiences. If you have a strong desire to learn a new language and experience a new culture, and are outgoing and like people, you possess the necessary characteristics to have a successful year.

Some exchange students are worried about everything they will miss out on at home while living abroad. But what you should really be concerned about is all you'll miss out on by *not* spending a year as an exchange student abroad!

Real-life experience
I have always been adventurous. Other cultures fascinate and inspire me. What fascinates me the most is how my meeting with a new culture, a new family, and new people has had such a huge impact on my perception of life. In the face of a new culture, I have gained a deeper understanding of who I am. Ironically, we sometimes need to travel across cultural boundaries to get to know ourselves!
—former exchange student to Australia

Making the Decision

Even if you are approved by an exchange organization, ultimately the only one who can tell whether you're ready for a year abroad is you! If you are not sure, do some more research before you make the decision. Call your exchange organization and get answers to any unanswered questions. Talk to former exchange students, friends, and family, and listen to what they say. Continue reading this book. Look inside yourself and ask why you want to be an exchange student. And ask yourself if you really understand what being an exchange student involves. Then, if you are still motivated and still have a burning desire to learn, discover, and meet new people, a year as an exchange student is probably right for you.

Travel advice

Are you very insecure? Write a list of the pros and cons of studying abroad on a piece of paper. It is easier to make a decision when you have everything laid out before you in writing.

Chapter 5

Frequently Asked Questions

Here are some questions students commonly ask when they are considering an exchange year abroad. Several themes discussed in these questions are covered more thoroughly in later chapters of this book.

When do I have to decide whether or not to take an exchange year abroad?
Of course, the most important thing is that you decide before the deadline. In general, from five to fifteen months in advance is recommended, and the sooner you make your decision, the better. You will have more time to prepare yourself, and your organization will have more time to find a suitable host family for you. Also keep in mind that for some popular destinations (host countries), there are more students wanting to go on exchange than there are host families ready to accommodate them. In these cases, students are often accepted on a first-come, first-served basis.

What courses do/can I take at school?
This depends on the country you wish to travel to. Some countries are known for offering students a wide range of classes, whereas other countries offer only a limited number. In addition, your organization or school may require you to take certain mandatory classes, such as the host country's language or history. Students still in high school who want to

have the year abroad count as a school year at home need to consult their home school for advice.

How do I get assigned to a host family?

Like exchange students, host families must apply and be interviewed in order to be approved. The exchange organizations then try to match students with host families. In the final round, however, the host family chooses the exchange student.

Can I change my host family?

Yes, but not just for any reason. If you are not getting along well with your host family, it is important that you try to find out why and, together with your family, try to solve any problems you may have. See chapter 18 for more information on this issue.

Can I visit home during the year?

Exchange students are usually not allowed to go home while participating in an exchange program. The reason for this is that going home can cause visa trouble and can also have a negative effect on the exchange experience. But there are exceptions to this rule. Talk with your organization about its policy. In the case of serious illness or death in the family, students are normally allowed to go home.

Can family and friends visit me while I am abroad?

A visit from home, especially if it occurs early in the exchange year, can trigger homesickness and have a negative impact on the experience. For that reason, some organizations recommend that students do not receive visits until the last half of the stay. Different organizations have different guidelines on this issue. Contact yours to find out. Also note that you cannot assume that your visitors will be staying with your host family. Your host family has already opened up their home to you, and it is unreasonable to expect them to do the same for your guests. Do not use your host family's house as a hotel for others.

I'll be traveling to the USA. May I take part in the graduation ceremony there?
It is up to each school to decide whether exchange students can participate in the graduation ceremony. Some schools allow it, whereas other schools restrict participation to students who are actually finishing their education at that particular school.

Test Yourself: Are You Ready for a School Year Abroad?

Choose the alternative (a, b, or c) that best describes you, and then add your points to get your total score.

	Score
1 Why do you want to be an exchange student? a) I don't. It's my parents' idea. (0 points) b) Mainly because I'm tired of home life and want to get away. (5 points) c) I'm curious about the world and want to experience a foreign culture. (10 points)	
2 What is the longest you have ever been away from your home and family? a) 4 days or less. (0) b) 5-10 days. (5) c) 10 days or more. (10)	
3 What kind of person are you? a) I am a very shy person who does not like to talk. (0) b) I can be a little shy, but I become more social when I feel comfortable. (5) c) I am social and outgoing. I seek contact with other people. (10)	
4 How picky are you about food? a) I am a very picky and do not like a lot of different foods. (0) b) There are some things I do not eat, but I usually try new things. (5) c) I eat (almost) everything and like to try new foods. I do not think I will have any problems getting used to different foods. (10)	
5 How do you like sports and group activities? a) I prefer sitting still. (0) b) I do some sports and/or activities. (5) c) I am very active and make the most of opportunities to participate in group activities. (10)	

6 How do you deal with other religions and beliefs? a) I'm not very comfortable around people with other religious beliefs. (0) b) I have never thought about it before. (5) c) I accept that some people have religious beliefs that are different than mine. (10)	
7 What kind of student are you? a) I am not very interested in school and often sleep in class. (0) b) I make an average effort to learn in school. (5) c) I'm very interested in my school work and try to be a serious student. (10)	
8 What is your relationship with foreign countries and cultures? a) I have no knowledge of foreign countries or cultures. (0) b) I have some knowledge of foreign countries and cultures. (5) c) I have broad knowledge of foreign countries and cultures. (10)	
9 How do you deal with challenges and difficult situations? a) Very poorly. I'm easily upset or frustrated. (0) b) Challenges and difficult situations are uncomfortable, but I face them. (5) c) I'm used to challenges and always try to make the best out of difficult situations. (10)	
10 How do you react to homesickness? a) I try to get home as quickly as possible. (0) b) I become sad and avoid people around me. (5) c) I try to think positively—I don't let homesickness ruin everything for me. (10)	

Total score: _____

Conclusion

0-30 points

Think carefully about your decision. Remember that as an exchange student, you'll be far from home in a foreign culture where you'll be expected to adapt. It is important to have realistic expectations for the year. If you're not ready for change, maybe it's best to stay home.

30-60 points

Take some time to familiarize yourself with what a year as an exchange student really means. Know yourself and make sure your expectations are realistic. Then, if you still want to travel, a school year abroad is probably right for you!

60-100 points

You're curious and positive—a natural exchange student. If you have decided to spend a school year abroad, we wish you a good trip and good luck!

Please note: This test is meant only as an indication of how suited you are for spending a school year abroad. It does not replace formal and personal assessment.

PART
2

PRE-DEPARTURE

Chapter 6

Choosing a Country
and an Exchange Organization

The first step on the road to becoming an exchange student is choosing a destination country and an exchange organization. Most countries have a wide selection of organizations that, combined, offer exchange to more than fifty other countries. Many students have some idea where they want to go and with what organization; others may be uncertain. Considering how many choices there are, it is no wonder that students often have a hard time making a decision!

Selecting a Country

The country you select will eventually have a major impact on your school year abroad. Therefore, choose your country carefully. Make sure it's one in which you really want to live. Having said that, many unexpected opportunities and hidden charms are found in the countries you know the least about. Many exchange students would be pleasantly surprised if they chose an *untraditional* host country such as the Czech Republic or Indonesia. For this very reason, several exchange organizations recommend that students think "outside the box" (unconventionally) when picking a host country.

Whatever country you choose, it is important to have realistic expectations about the country you select. It is fine to be a cowboy fan, but if you choose to visit the USA because you expect to live on a ranch, you will easily be disappointed. Do not make your decision by throwing darts at a world map. Instead, try to find out which countries seem interesting to you and then try to learn more about them.

Fun fact—Did you know that . . .
dinnertime can vary greatly from country to country? In Germany, for example, people usually eat dinner around noon; in the USA, around six o'clock in the evening; and in Spain, as late as ten at night!

Do Not Forget the Language

The language of the host country is just as important as the country itself. Learning the host country's language during your stay is crucial for your success. You will use this language at school, to speak to your host family, to make friends, and to avoid misunderstandings.

If you are motivated to master the language, the actual learning process will be easier. Moreover, the better you become in the language, the better your chances are of having a successful year. It is one thing to travel to a country whose language you already know, and quite different to travel to one with a language that's completely new to you. If you go to a country whose language is different from yours, you will have to be extra motivated because it takes a lot of effort and practice to learn to speak, read, and write in a new language. Therefore, make sure you choose a country with a language you really want to learn.

Fun fact—Did you know that . . .
the English word *window* comes from the Old
Norwegian word *vindauge*, meaning "wind eye"?
The "wind eye" was a hole in the wall used for
looking outside. If you put your eye up to the hole,
you could feel the wind blowing into your eye, and
that's how it got the name "wind eye."

Different Languages

Some languages are more difficult to learn than others. For
many Westerners, a rule of thumb is that it takes three times
longer to become fluent in Chinese than in French. In other
words, a Brazilian student should not expect to be as fluent
in Mandarin Chinese after a year in China as he or she would
be in English after a year in Great Britain. However, fluency
might not be your main goal for the exchange year.

How to Choose a Host Country

Make a list of the countries you find interesting, and then use
the Internet or a library to search for information about them.
You can also read about different countries on the websites
of exchange organizations. It is also a good idea to get advice
from other people, especially former exchange students.
Listen to their experiences and opinions. However, in the end,
you must select a country in which you would like to live and
whose language you would like to learn.

Fun fact—Did you know that . . .
in most countries, people drive on the right side
of the road, but in some countries, such as India,
Great Britain, Japan, and Australia, people drive on
the left side?

Exchange Organizations

The exchange organization's job is to accept students, enroll them in a school, provide a host family, help with visas, book flight tickets, prepare the student for life abroad, and offer support throughout the year.

The main difference among the many exchange organizations is how well they perform these functions. Their abilities to match families with students and to provide support throughout the year can vary greatly.

How Do I Choose an Exchange Organization?

You should become familiar with the organization before you choose it, and feel confident that its staff members will do their best to help you before and during your stay abroad. You can learn about exchange organizations by visiting their websites, ordering their brochures, and talking with former exchange students who have used their services. In addition, it is a good idea to go to informational meetings, to call or send an e-mail requesting more detailed information, and to ask specific questions. Ask how they select exchange students, how they find host families, how much their programs cost, how they prepare students for the year abroad, and how they follow up with them once they are settled in their host countries.

Notice how each organization responds to your questions. Do its representatives really answer them? Do they give detailed answers, or short ones? How long does it take them to respond to your e-mails? When you compare program prices, remember to see what is included and what is not. Also, make sure that your organization is professionally run and holds the standard certification and other typical accreditations in your home country.

> **Travel advice**
> Familiarize yourself with different exchange organizations, compare them, and select the one that best meets your needs.

List of Organizations

Every country has its own set of exchange organizations. Below is a list of some of the largest and oldest worldwide exchange organizations. To find more organizations, look online or see if your school counselor or library has any brochures.

AFS Intercultural Programs
AFS.org
Established: 1946

EF Education First
EF.com
Established: 1965

Rotary Youth Exchange
Rotary.org
Established: 1972
Note: Exchange through Rotary is organized through local Rotary clubs. Locate your closest Rotary Club for more information.

YFU (Youth for Understanding)
YFU.org
Established: 1951

Chapter 7

Application, Interview, and Paperwork

In order to be approved as an exchange student, you will need to go through an application and interview process. Once you have been approved, you will need to complete some additional paperwork before you can travel. This may take some time, but your exchange organization will assist you throughout the process.

The Application

The application form is designed to help the organization get to know you better and will be the basis for finding you a host family. Moreover, it will serve as the first "meeting" between you and your prospective contact person and host family, so you need to make a good first impression!

Take your time when filling out your application. Answer each question thoroughly. If you are filling out the form by hand (as opposed to online) you may wish to make a copy of the form and write a draft first. If you must fill out your application in a language you do not know well (e.g., the host country's language), ask a language teacher at your school to look over your answers. Good language use always helps give a positive impression.

Travel advice
If you have to write a letter to your prospective host family as part of the application, don't just write about your activities and hobbies in your home country. Also include activities or hobbies that you would like to try out that are connected to your prospective host country (e.g., curling in Canada, baseball in the USA, rugby in Ireland, etc.).

Travel advice
Choose a good picture for your application. A picture says more than a thousand words!

Be Honest!

Do not write or say anything that is not true in your application or during your interview. The host family will be selected partly on the basis of what you write about yourself. If you are not truthful, you could end up with a host family you will not fit in with.

Travel advice
Spend time on your application. Try to bring out your best qualities, but be honest! If possible, get someone else to proofread your application, especially if it will be used to find you a host family.

The Interview

The interview gives your exchange organization an opportunity to meet you face to face so that they can form a better impression of you as a person. It also gives you a valuable opportunity to ask questions about your possible trip abroad. The person conducting the interview will write an assessment which, together with your application, will be used to determine whether you will be admitted to the exchange program.

Travel advice
Make sure that you show up to your interview on time. Then relax and stay positive. Most important, show that you are motivated and open to new ideas and experiences.

If You Are Rejected

If you are rejected, you should talk to the exchange organization to find out why. Make sure to apply early so that in case of rejection you'll have time to apply to another exchange organization. Having a backup plan is always a smart idea.

Other Paperwork

After you have been approved by an exchange organization, there are some formalities you'll need to take care of. These include making sure you have the required health certificates, visas, proof of immunization, travel insurance, and references. This will involve some time and effort on your part. Do not hesitate to ask your exchange organization for help if you feel you need it.

Travel advice

Fill out and take care of all paperwork as soon as possible. Do not wait until the last minute! The sooner you finish, the faster your organization can start looking for a suitable host family for you. You will also have more time to prepare mentally for the upcoming experience, and you will avoid possible stress.

Travel advice

Before sending in your paperwork, make copies and put them in a binder or folder for easy reference.

Chapter 8

Preparations

Some exchange students feel that too much preparation will somehow take away much of the surprise and excitement associated with moving to a foreign country. This is completely untrue. There is far more to a year abroad than what you can read in a book! Good preparation will not destroy or reduce any of the experiences and discoveries that lie ahead of you. On the contrary, it will help you avoid disappointment, misunderstandings, and embarrassing situations. Preparation will make you better equipped to face challenges, problems, and difficult situations. On the whole, good preparation will provide you with the best possible foundation for a successful year.

Mental Preparation

Attitude

If you are willing to do only one thing to prepare for your year abroad, let it be this: work on your attitude! Your attitude will undoubtedly be the most important factor in determining how much you get out of being an exchange student. Remember that unrealistically high expectations may lead to disappointment. Try to be open to new experiences and enjoy the fact that you will be encountering completely new situations, practices, and people.

Change

Living with a host family and studying abroad will likely be the greatest challenge in your life so far! Be prepared to adapt to a new lifestyle, including a different climate, unusual food, and unfamiliar people. You may need to wake up earlier than you do at home. Perhaps you will not have the same level of Internet access or mobile phone service that you are used to having. You may have to share a bedroom with a host sibling. Or you may have to bicycle to school rather than being driven there. Whatever happens, life will definitely be different for you!

Travel advice
Lower your expectations and prepare yourself for something completely different. Be cooperative and ready to adapt.

Travel advice
Before you travel, write a letter to yourself. This is a good way to prepare yourself mentally, and later it will show you how much you have changed during the year. Write about your expectations of your host country, what you think you will miss about home, your best friend, your favorite food—anything about yourself. Put the letter in an envelope and leave it in a drawer until you return from your exchange year.

Host Country

Before you travel, learn a bit about your host country, its people, and its culture. This will help you to understand more of what's around you. This will also make you feel more confident, and enable you to learn even more while you are there. This kind of preparation will also make it easier to adjust to your new home. It will help you to take part in a greater range of conversations and to avoid misunderstandings. In addition, it will give others a good impression of you, because you will show that you are interested in their society and culture. It will also allow you to take part in a greater range of conversations.

Fun fact—Did you know that . . .
in many countries in Southeast Asia, not looking someone in the eyes when you talk to them is a way to show respect?

Read through the material that your exchange organization sends you, search the Internet or borrow a book. Talk to former exchange students and read their blogs or letters about their journeys.

Fun fact—Did you know that . . .
in many countries it is considered very rude to call a person by his or her first name unless you have been given permission to do so?

Your Home Country

People in your host country will ask questions about your home country, and some of the questions may be about your country's political system, culture, history, or current issues. Being able to intelligently answer these questions will give you respect, so reading a little bit about your own country before you go might be a good idea, as well.

Language Preparation

One of the most important factors for having a successful year is communication. The more you can speak and understand your host country's language, the better you will be able to make yourself understood. Speaking the language will help you find new friends, take part in daily life, and study at school. Once you are able to express yourself properly, you will feel more comfortable and better enjoy your stay.

You might wonder why you should start learning the host country's language before you travel. After all, won't you learn the language while you are there? Of course you will! But if you leave for your host country without knowing any words in advance, you're likely to spend an enormous amount of time feeling confused and insecure. The language will take longer to learn, and your learning in general will probably go much more slowly. Compare the process with how you learned mathematics: first you learned how to count, then how to write numbers, and then what the plus and minus signs meant. Only then could you begin solving math problems. What if you hadn't learned the basics first, and someone had just pushed a sheet of math problems in front of you? You might have come to recognize certain patterns eventually, and in the end you would even have learned to do some mathematics. But it would have taken much longer without the preparation, and it would not have been a pleasant or easy way to learn!

Fun fact—Did you know that . . .
in Thailand there are more than a dozen words for
the word *you*?

It is important to know the basics of your host country's language before you travel. This is especially true if English is rarely used there. Without knowing the basics of the local language, you will struggle to make yourself understood, and it may take an unnecessarily long time to learn the host country's language. And in the meantime, there is a good chance that you will feel frustrated or perhaps even homesick and mildly depressed.

Fun fact—Did you know that . . .
South Africa has eleven official languages?

So start preparing today! Learn the alphabet or the most basic written signs that are used in your host country. Try to learn as many words as possible, especially some of the most common verbs and nouns, as well as some useful phrases. This will allow you to make a smoother transition when you arrive and will help you learn the language more quickly and easily. You will speak the language much more fluently at the end of the exchange year if you start learning it before you go.

Even if you're going to Great Britain, the USA, or another English-speaking country, you will be at a considerable advantage if you work on your English before you go. Therefore, start practicing as early as possible. Locate a book in English or set up English speech and/or subtitles the next time you watch a movie at home.

Travel advice
Learn as much as possible about the host country's language before you travel.

Proposed Language Training

- Talk to a language teacher at your school or look for books that you can use to start learning the language.

- Watch videos with speech and subtitles in the host country's language.
- Read texts or books that are appropriate to your language level, such as children's books, youth novels, or newspapers.
- Create flash cards of commonly used words. Put the foreign word on one side and the translation on the other.
- Put stick-on notes on common objects (your chair, table, bed, closet, door, window, etc.) with their names in the host country's language.
- Look for language training and testing websites.
- If the host country's language is completely new to you, sign up for an evening course or find someone who can teach you a little.

Travel advice
Do you find it boring to learn language in the traditional way? Try programs like Pimsleur Language or Rosetta Stone.

Travel advice
Keep some flash cards (see above) in your pocket and use them whenever you have some spare time, such as when you're on the bus or waiting in line.

Practical Preparations

Before you travel, there are three particular matters you should think about:

Money abroad

First, decide how you will manage your money while you're abroad. In most cases, it will be sufficient to bring an internationally recognized credit or debit card like Visa or MasterCard. With such a card, you can withdraw money at virtually any ATM (automatic teller (cash) machine). An alternative is to open a bank account abroad and get someone at home to transfer money to it. You can also bring traveler's checks, exchange sufficient money for foreign currency before you go, or bring cash in an internationally recognized currency, such as US dollars, and then exchange it locally. Keep in mind, however, that carrying a lot of cash is always risky and that traveler's checks are not accepted everywhere. In any case, make sure you compare exchange and bank fees to get the best and cheapest solution.

Staying in touch with home

Second, decide how you will keep in touch with home. One good method is Skype (Skype.com), which offers free calls over the Internet. Also, you may be able to buy an overseas calling card that lets you call home from any phone, without the owner of the phone paying more than the local rate.

Mobile phone

Third, find out what it costs to use your mobile phone abroad. The cost often varies depending on which provider you select in the host country. When you arrive at your host country, get a local SIM card/mobile number to make it easier and cheaper to keep in touch with your host family and new friends. Make sure that your mobile phone has not been locked by your provider at home.

Suggested Checklist—Practical Preparation

☐ Inform your school about your exchange year and discuss any possible issues.

☐ Check that your passport is valid and in a good physical condition.

☐ Obtain a valid visa.

☐ Buy travel insurance.

☐ Find out if you need any new vaccines/immunizations.

☐ Plan how you'll manage your money abroad.

☐ Decide how you will stay in touch with your family at home.

☐ Purchase a gift for your host family.

☐ Return any borrowed items.

☐ Familiarize yourself with the rules and regulations of your exchange organization.

Travel advice

Read Dale Carnegie's *How to Win Friends and Influence People*. It has sold more than fifteen million copies worldwide. This book teaches you how to socialize more successfully, and it will help you both as an exchange student and in life in general.

Chapter 9

Packing: What Should I Bring?

Packing your suitcase will probably be one of the most enjoyable preparations. Nevertheless, knowing what to bring is not always easy. Carefully consider what you take with you.

Before you start packing, find out about your baggage allowance—in particular, the number of suitcases you can carry and the weight restriction. Usually the allowance is one suitcase weighing 20-23 kg (44-50 lb.). You may also be allowed to carry additional suitcases for an extra charge. Once you have your plane tickets, you can find this out on the airline's website, or you can ask your exchange organization.

Travel advice
Do not wait until the last day to begin packing! Packing your suitcase for a whole year will probably take longer than you expect. Start thinking about what you want to bring at least two weeks in advance.

Don't worry if there is some space left in your suitcase after you've finished packing. During your exchange year, you will probably acquire many different things, so any free space will come in handy for your flight home.

Clothing

Deciding what clothes to bring depends on one thing—where you are going! There are two factors to consider here: climate and culture. Go online to find out about the climate where you will be staying. Consider the seasonal temperatures and weather. Will you need to bring clothes for snow and cold weather, or is your host country hot most of the time? Also, make sure the clothes you are planning on bringing are considered suitable in your host country. For example, most Western countries are very easygoing about girls' clothing that reveals the waistline and lower neck, whereas some other countries are not. And in Thailand, you wouldn't want to wear anything orange—that color is reserved for Buddhist monks.

Travel advice

If you are going to a country where clothes are cheaper than (or the same price as) at home, do not spend a lot of money buying new clothes before you leave. Wait until you are in your host country. That way, you can see and buy what other kids your age are wearing. You'll fit in more easily and you'll save some money!

Gift for Your Host Family

It is common for exchange students to give their host family a small gift to show gratitude for their hospitality. The gift does not need to be expensive—it's the thought that counts. Consider giving them something typical of your home country, for example a book or a T-shirt from your city, region, or country. If the family has young children, it might be a good idea to bring some traditional candy from your country.

Travel advice

If you have some room left in your suitcase, why not bring a few extra gifts? During your year abroad, you may want to show gratitude to some other people, as well. Giving them something from your home country is a unique way to show your appreciation.

Photo Album

Your host family will definitely be interested in looking at pictures of your life at home. So bring along a small photo album with pictures of you, your family, your friends, your pet, etc. Include some pictures of everyday things like your classroom, a grocery store, or public transportation. If you don't have the time (or space) to bring a photo album, find some interesting pictures and put them in a folder on your computer or on a memory stick. Or you can just print them out and bring them with you. It's cheap, easy, and fast, and your host family will definitely enjoy the pictures!

Special Items

If you're thinking of bringing with you a large or fragile musical instrument, a piece of sports equipment, or a hobby item, stop and consider whether you really need it. Perhaps you should use the year to try something new. On the other hand, if it is an important part of your life, it is probably worth sharing with your new family. If so, find out if it would be easier and cheaper to buy, rent, or borrow what you need in your host country. If you do decide to bring an instrument or another large object, check with the airline to find out how feasible it is to do so. Airlines often have special rules covering instruments and sports equipment, and they may charge extra. An alternative is to have the item sent to you by mail.

Suggested Packing List

- ☐ clothes
- ☐ formalwear for special occasions
- ☐ shoes (for practical use)
- ☐ nice shoes for special occasions
- ☐ toiletries
- ☐ special medication (if needed)
- ☐ dictionary
- ☐ this book
- ☐ camera
- ☐ mobile phone
- ☐ copies of important papers (visas, passports, application, regulations, etc.)
- ☐ album with pictures that you can show your host family and others
- ☐ iPod or MP3 player
- ☐ laptop (if you have one)
- ☐ book with pictures from your home country
- ☐ music from your home country (which can be played for others in the host country)
- ☐ gift for your host family
- ☐ power adapter

Power Adapter

Your host country may not use the same electrical outlets or voltage as your home country. If you plan to bring electronic devices such as a laptop or mobile phone charger, do some research about the outlets and voltage ahead of time. AC adapters can be purchased at airports and travel shops.

Travel advice
Mark your luggage with your name and address.
To make your suitcases easier to spot, you can add
some stickers or colored tape.

Hand Luggage

Before you travel, find out how much and what you can
carry in your hand luggage (carry-on). As a rule of thumb,
the airline will require you to put everything of great value,
such as laptops, jewelry, and cameras, in your hand luggage.
In addition, other things you may need during the trip, such
as a book or a sweatshirt, should be packed in your hand
luggage.

Checklist for hand luggage

- ☐ your passport and visa
- ☐ your flight tickets and travel documents
- ☐ a document with the address and contact information
  of your host family and/or contact person abroad
- ☐ a fully charged mobile phone with sufficient air time/
  prepaid minutes
- ☐ a small dictionary (for non-English-speaking countries)
- ☐ a little cash in the host country's currency, if possible
- ☐ items that must be carried in your hand luggage, as
  specified by your airline (camera, laptop, etc.)

Running Out of Room?

If you are struggling to find space for everything you want
to bring, sort out the most important items and pack them
first. Then leave out anything you can purchase in your host

country. Shampoo, conditioner, and notebooks, for example, can easily be bought abroad. Then, set aside items that you would use very rarely. Hiking boots, for example, can be left at home, unless you know you're going hiking during weekends and holidays. If you still have items that you would like to bring but that won't fit into your luggage, consider mailing them to your host country at a later point.

Travel advice

If you are unsure whether or not you will need something, put it in a (cardboard) box at home. That way, your parents can easily mail it to you should you need it.

Chapter 10

Departure

The departure day is very exciting—you are just hours away from your new life and family! It is not unusual to have mixed feelings on this day. On the one hand, you are sad about leaving friends and family. On the other hand, you are looking forward to everything that is awaiting you in your host country. Whatever your feelings, now is the time to keep your head up and look forward, because this is when your adventure begins.

The Last Days before Departure

If you are smart, you will do your packing and get everything ready well ahead of time. That way you will avoid stress on the final days before departure. In addition, you will be able to spend the last days before departure doing something enjoyable. You could invite some friends over, go out and do something fun, or simply eat out with your family. In any case, it is advantageous to be well-rested on the day of departure.

Travel advice
Do something enjoyable on the day before you travel to your new home.

Farewell Party

A going-away party is a great way to say good-bye to friends. However, the party does not have to be on the very last night before you leave, especially if you have to get up very early to catch your plane.

Jet Lag

If you are crossing several time zones, you might experience jet lag. Many people don't worry about jet lag, but if you want to minimize the effects, try these tips:

1. Get enough sleep the night before you travel—a rested body can handle jet lag better.
2. Drink plenty of water before and during the journey.
3. If you have the opportunity, you can ease the transition to a new time zone by gradually advancing or delaying your bedtime during the days before departure—going to bed earlier if you are traveling west and later if you're traveling east.

The Day of Travel

Finally—the big day has arrived, and your last hours in your home country are coming to an end.

This is not the day to oversleep: you want to allow yourself plenty of time to get to the airport. Set two alarm clocks, and if you are driving to the airport, allow time for traffic jams, parking, etc. If you are traveling by train or bus, familiarize yourself with the relevant timetables and try not to catch the last available train, in case of unforeseen delays. Finally, remember to check to see that you have not left anything behind!

> **Travel advice**
> Wear something nice and appropriate on the day of departure (nothing offensive or revealing). It will help you make a good first impression on your host family/contact person.

Check-In

Make sure you have marked your luggage with your name and phone number before you hand it over at the airport. (Tags are available near the check-in counter.) If you are changing flights several times, ask whether the luggage will be sent directly to your final destination or whether you must pick it up on your own and check it in again. When you're done checking in, you will get a luggage receipt in addition to your boarding pass. This is usually a small piece of paper with a bar code on it. Take good care of it! You will need it in case something happens to your luggage.

Changing Flights

Most exchange students have to change flights at least once. If you have less than three hours until your next flight, find the departure gate and go there immediately. Many airports are so big that you will need to take a bus to get from one terminal to another. Extra security checks and passport controls may take a long time, too. Postpone shopping and eating until you have found your new gate.

The same principle applies if you need to travel by train or bus from the airport. As soon as you land, find out where the relevant station, bus stop, or track is located. That way, you will avoid stress and minimize the risk of missing your connection.

Travel advice
Go directly to your next gate at stopovers/layovers.

Real-life experience
I thought I had plenty of time when I got to the airport in Frankfurt. It was, after all, more than two hours until my flight to the United States would take off, but an unexpected security check with the longest queue I've ever seen meant that I barely got into the aircraft before the scheduled departure time. The strange thing is that the same thing happened at the airport in Washington, DC, on the way home!
    —former exchange student to New York, USA

Arrival

Once you've arrived at your destination, you will be greeted by your new host family or contact person. Even if you're very tired, try to be positive when you are greeted. First impressions do count a lot.

Travel advice
Smile when you meet your contact person and host family for the first time.

If Your Bags Do Not Appear on the Baggage Belt

1. First check that you are standing by the correct baggage belt.
2. Wait until the message "last bag on belt" (or something similar) appears on the screen.

3. Go to the baggage claim counter (usually located near the baggage belt). You will need the receipt that you received at check-in (the bar code sticker). The staff there will help you. If your suitcase does not arrive with your plane, it's usually the airline's responsibility to forward the baggage to the address where you are staying, free of charge.

If Your Baggage Is Damaged

The chances that your luggage will be damaged during the transit are very low. However, if it does happen, contact the airline's service desk. Get the staff to confirm that your baggage is damaged. Unless you do this, you will not be able to request compensation later—neither from your travel insurance nor from the airline. Further, ask the airline how they will compensate you for the damage and what steps you should take to request compensation.

In Case of Delay

If one of your flights is delayed and you miss your connecting flight, go to the airline's service counter. The people there will try their best to get you on the next available flight. Also, remember to call your host family, contact person, or exchange organization to let them know that you will not be arriving as planned.

PART
3

ABROAD

Chapter 11

About Being an Exchange Student

Your time as an exchange student will definitely be a unique chapter in your life. Once you have decided which country to visit, the framework for this new chapter is set. But the story itself—how exciting it is, what turns it takes, and what you do and experience—is still up to you. You are its main character and its author at the same time. Your choices, your attitude, and what you make of your time there determine how exciting and successful your experience will be. No matter how your story unfolds, it will be most extraordinary!

A Growing Experience

You grow a lot as a person when you're an exchange student and have to be more independent than you are at home. It is a year of maturing, and you will learn more about yourself and gain many new perspectives on life.

Real-life experience
I wish you a wonderful year! You are lucky to have the opportunity to go on exchange, and this is an experience you will never forget!
— former exchange student
to New Hampshire, USA

New Situations, New Roles

Until now you have felt confident in who you are and where you come from. You may be the youngest child in your family at home, or perhaps you are an only child. You have felt a natural part of your community, and you are used to living a certain way.

As an exchange student, however, you'll take on new roles. At school and in the community, you may be known as "the exchange student," and in your host family, you may be the oldest of five siblings.

This is what's so exciting about being an exchange student. You get to experience something that you otherwise would not have experienced. Maybe your host family lives in an apartment or on a farm. Maybe they have a sailboat, or maybe they don't even own a car. Perhaps students at your new school wear a uniform, or perhaps you may choose to take unusual class subjects like tourism, dance, or photography.

No matter what your year offers, seize every opportunity. Be open and positive. Try to make all your new experiences good ones!

A Fresh Start

In many ways, arriving in your host country represents a fresh start in life. Regardless of how you have been seen back home—rich or poor, northerner or southerner—the labels do not follow you to your host country. People there will also form an impression of you, but you'll have a new opportunity to introduce yourself in a new light.

Ambassador Role

As an exchange student, you are a kind of ambassador for your country. Many of the people you meet might never have met anyone from your home country before. Therefore, they will assume that what you do is how people typically behave in your country. The ambassador role is often more significant if you come to a smaller community. The less contact your community has had with foreigners, the more important your role as an ambassador will be. In any case, you should strive to act like a good ambassador for your country.

Travel advice
Don't write anything negative about your new community or host family on Facebook or other social media. This shows a lack of good character and judgment on your part, and chances are it will come back to haunt you.

Ups and Downs

All exchange students experience ups and downs throughout the year. These ups and downs may not come at the same time for all exchange students, but they will come. No two days are ever the same at home, either. But when you are on exchange, your feelings are typically stronger, so you'll experience both the good and the bad days more intensely. The figure below shows what the ups and downs of an exchange student's mood can look like. Your year might not play out exactly like this, but you should expect intense changes in mood and atmosphere so that you are prepared when they come.

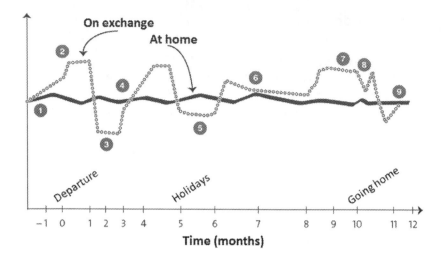

1. **Before departure**: You are looking forward to the exchange year.
2. **Arrival**: All the new sights and sounds are overwhelming. You are having a great time.
3. **Culture shock**: The honeymoon is over. Not everything feels like it did at first.
4. **Adjustment**: You have become accustomed to the host country and are beginning to make good friends.
5. **Holidays**: You miss your family back home.
6. **Halfway**: The year is halfway over and you are well integrated.
7. **The last months**: You have good friends and speak the language well. You are very well accustomed to life and enjoying it.
8. **Readjustment**: You must adapt to life at home again.
9. **Back home again**: You have adapted to life back home.

Now that you know that an exchange year contains ups and downs, exploit it! Fully enjoy the good times, and when times get tough, keep your spirits high and think positively. You can never appreciate the sunshine without a little rain from time to time.

The First Weeks

The first weeks will probably be among the most exciting for you as an exchange student. Everything is new: new country, new people, new language, new foods, new start, new experiences—no wonder it can take some time getting used to life! It is normal to be extremely excited about going to school, but don't expect this feeling to last throughout the year. Schoolwork and assignments will gradually bring you back to earth, but enjoy the excitement while it lasts!

Staying in Touch with Home

It has become inexpensive and easy to keep in touch with people in other countries. Through e-mail, Skype, and social networking sites like Facebook, getting a general idea of what's happening at home doesn't require a major effort.

It is natural to want to keep in touch with family and friends back home, but if you spend too much time doing it, it will have a negative impact on your stay. Some exchange students get so absorbed in using Skype or Facebook that they completely forget the purpose of their stay. If you make daily phone calls to your parents or spend hours in front of the computer chatting with your friends back home, you'll be losing valuable time that should be spent making new friends or forming a good relationship with your host family.

Too much contact with family and old friends can trigger homesickness. It can also give your host family the impression that you are unhappy there. Try to limit your contact with people at home to an appropriate level. Several phone calls home a day is too much.

Real-life experience

I believe that modern communication is both a blessing and a curse for foreign exchange students nowadays. I was an exchange student in southwestern Missouri back in 1991-92, when the Internet and cheap calls did not exist. The letters I wrote to my friends took about two weeks to arrive, and I spoke to my family at home every two months. Of course, it was sometimes hard not to know what was happening at home, but I had one huge advantage: no one back home was expecting me to call or chat with them. This allowed me to focus 100 percent on becoming a part of life in my host country.

— former exchange student to Missouri, USA

Real-life experience

It has been my experience that exchange students who spend much of their free time conversing with natural family and friends back home in their native language typically *do not* improve their English skills as quickly as those who don't. I advise students to e-mail with family frequently, but Skype or call no more than once a week.

— regional exchange student coordinator
in New York, USA

Your Contact Person

Your contact person is there to help you get the most out of your year. If you have any questions, worries, or difficulties that you don't feel like discussing with your host family, the contact person is probably the right one to go to. However, you should be aware that most contact people are volunteers, with their own family and usually a full-time job. They often get little or no pay for their work as a contact person. You should therefore not expect them to be available twenty-four hours a day. (For urgent matters or emergencies, it is often better to call the dedicated emergency number provided by your exchange organization.)

Most contact people also appreciate hearing from exchange students when things are going well or when there is "nothing to tell." Send an e-mail or make a phone call once in a while to tell your contact person how you are doing, and send him or her a postcard if you go away on a trip.

Spending Money

Exchange students who travel to countries where things are less expensive than in their home country may be tempted to spend too much money. But spending more than other kids your age may have unfortunate consequences. For one thing, it can have a negative impact on your image, making you seem spoiled. What's more, excessive spending creates an awkward gap between you and your friends, making it harder to form good relationships with them.

If you like spending money, therefore, put some of your shopping bags inside larger ones when you're shopping. That way it looks as though you have bought a little less than you actually did. And don't show off everything you buy. You should especially refrain from telling others how much an expensive purchase cost. Also, don't keep more cash in your wallet than what is normal among your friends.

Travel advice
Be careful not to spend too much money openly.
When you're with others, do not spend more money
than they do.

Mobile Phone

You should get a new mobile number in your host country. That makes it easier and cheaper to contact your host family and friends, and it also makes it cheaper to send text messages and call home. Even if you do not mind paying €2 or $2 a minute, remember that those who are going to call and text you will want to avoid that sort of high charge.

Safety

It is relatively safe to be an exchange student. In fact, you may find that your host parents—just in order to keep you safe—are stricter with you than with your host siblings. Your host family or contact person will let you know about any safety precautions you must take. In addition, there are some general measures that will help prevent something undesirable from happening:

- Have the phone number of your host family with you at all times. If you have trouble memorizing it, write it down on a piece of paper and keep it with you.
- Learn the emergency number for your host country.
- Always carry your mobile phone when you leave home.
- Carry your insurance card in your wallet or bag. Take it with you wherever you go.
- Do not go out alone at night.
- Hide the keypad when you enter your debit card's PIN number.
- Do not carry a lot of cash with you.
- If you travel through a questionable neighborhood or walk by a suspicious-looking group of people, do not act insecure or nervous. Do not look all around you as if you are a tourist. Act confident and you will become a less likely target.

- Do not give details about yourself to people you don't trust or know very well.
- If you decide to change sidewalks to avoid suspicious-looking people, do it before you get near them.

Fun fact—Did you know . . .
some countries, such as India, Iran, and Venezuela, do not follow the "full hour" of their time zones? When the time is 12:00 in continental Europe, it is 16:30 in India, 07:30 in Venezuela, and 14:30 in Iran.

Chapter 12

Living in a Foreign Culture

Becoming immersed in a foreign culture is what student exchange is all about. Feeling comfortable in the new culture, being able to communicate properly with others, and becoming integrated into the community are important to the success of your exchange year. But sometimes it is difficult to notice and adapt to cultural differences.

Developing Intercultural Competence

What we perceive as rude, unacceptable, proper, polite, or necessary behavior is based on the many cultural values and norms that we have been taught since birth. For example, spitting on the sidewalk is unacceptable in some cultures but perfectly fine in others. Judging people's actions based upon your home culture is okay—as long as you stay home. Problems arise when you are in a foreign country and you judge members of that culture based on the rules and norms of your home culture. Unfortunately, this is a very natural thing to do. Even when you travel to a foreign culture, your own cultural baggage stays with you, and it can often lead to uncomfortable situations.

But in order to understand a culture, feel comfortable in it, and communicate effectively with people from it, you have to suspend judgment. Do not immediately interpret others' actions in terms of your own home culture. In many cultures, for example, holding the thumb up means "everything is okay," whereas in others it signifies the number one, and still in others, it is a rude sexual sign. You need to accept differences and new approaches. The ability to recognize, understand and successfully deal with cultural differences is called *intercultural competence*. Next we will lay out some ways to help you develop that ability.

Not Wrong—Just Different

The first step toward intercultural competence is acknowledging that there are no inherent cultural rights or wrongs. There are just differences. For example, in the USA it is common to shower standing upright in the bathtub, whereas in Indonesia, you shower by pouring water over your head with a ladle. Unfortunately, we tend to use ourselves and our own culture as a measure when evaluating other cultures. This means that we judge other cultures as either better or worse—and more often as worse.

If you are constantly searching for things in your host country's culture that you think are worse than your own, you will only succeed in offending people. You will appear unmotivated and not very adaptable—not the image you want to portray. Constantly perceiving things in a negative light will only work against you. Remind yourself that there is no one correct way to eat, greet other people, show emotions, or communicate with others. There are several ways of doing all these things, and each of them is just as right as the other.

Fun fact—Did you know that . . .
in Thailand, everything that depicts the king, such as money, is treated with the utmost respect and care? For example, using your shoe to stop a rolling coin (which carries the king's image) is seen as disrespectful and degrading.

Spotting Cultural Differences

The second step to developing intercultural competence is acknowledging that most differences are hard to spot. We smell, see, hear, and touch, and therefore we think we see all the cultural differences, but most of them are not so obvious. It can be a challenge to learn the unwritten norms and rules of a new country. In some cultures, making a joke about someone's appearance is insulting, whereas in other cultures it is okay. In a way, any culture is like an iceberg. Some parts of the culture are observable to the eye (the top of the iceberg), but most of it is not (the part of the iceberg that is underwater). Knowing how to dress for a certain occasion is something you can observe by looking at what other people are wearing. But knowing which types of jokes are considered funny and which are offensive is not so obvious.

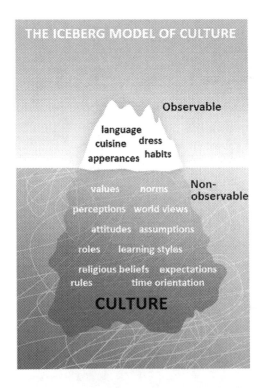

THE ICEBERG MODEL OF CULTURE

Observable

language
cuisine   dress
apperances   habits

Non-observable

values   norms
perceptions   world views
attitudes   assumptions
roles   learning styles
religious beliefs   expectations
rules   time orientation

CULTURE

Because it can be hard to see cultural differences, you should constantly be on the lookout for them. In parts of the Arab world, for example, it's perfectly normal for two men who know each other well to hold hands while walking; in other cultures, this is less common. When encountering situations that seem wrong or weird to you, stop and ask yourself whether it could simply be a case of cultural difference.

Dealing with Insecurity and Negative Situations

The third and final step in developing intercultural competence is dealing with situations that make you feel insecure or offended. You need to learn to put aside your own cultural norms when you feel someone is being rude, offensive, aggressive, or inappropriate. An American citizen in Portugal might be shocked to see beer being served at McDonald's restaurants, because this would probably be considered inappropriate in the USA. If you feel that someone has done something inappropriate or offensive, stop for a bit and put yourself in his or her shoes. Consider the possibility that a cultural difference has come into play. Wait before you act, and seek advice from someone in that culture who is easy to talk to.

Examples of Value Differences

Collectivism vs. individualism

Some cultures value individualism and freedom of choice, whereas others value the well-being of the group over individual needs. In his book *The Geography of Thought*, Richard Nisbett notes that "East Asians live in an interdependent world in which the individual is part of a larger whole;

Westerners live in a world in which the individual is a unitary free agent."

Perceptions about time

Imagine you've agreed to meet a group of friends in a park on a Saturday at two o'clock in the afternoon. When would you show up? If you are German, you might answer, "A little earlier than two," whereas if you are Brazilian, you might answer, "I'd come at three." Now, imagine that German guy being an exchange student in Brazil. He shows up at the park at two o'clock and finds himself completely alone. He waits for forty-five minutes and then heads home, frustrated that his new Brazilian friends didn't show up. Imagine a Brazilian guy being an exchange student in Germany. He shows up at three o'clock and finds his German peers angry with him because he's an hour late.

Different cultures have different perspectives about time. In some cultures, showing up twenty minutes late for an appointment is considered disrespectful; in other cultures, it's perfectly normal.

The role of religion

In some cultures and for many individuals, religion is involved in all aspects of life, whereas other cultures and their people regard religion as a very private matter. Making a joke about religion is considered okay by some individuals and incredibly offensive by others.

Harmony vs. fairness

In some cultures, debate, arguments, and open confrontation are a normal part of life. Other cultures value harmony. Richard Nisbett notes in his book *The Geography of Thought* that "Easterners are highly attuned to the feelings of others and strive for interpersonal harmony; Westerners are more concerned with knowing themselves and are prepared to sacrifice harmony for fairness."

Cleanliness and hygiene

In many parts of Asia, a wet bathroom floor is considered clean and a dry floor possibly dirty. A Westerner would probably think the opposite. In some cultures, eating greasy food with your hands is perceived as unhygienic and disgusting, whereas in others, eating all sorts of food with your hands is customary. Different cultures have different perceptions of what is clean and hygienic.

Chapter 13

Fundamentals for a Successful Year

As an exchange student, you must be proactive in order to take full advantage of your experience abroad. Some situations may be determined completely by chance, but you are in control of more than you think.

There are some personal attributes and characteristics that will help you have a successful year. These relate to preparation, attitude, observation, communication, interest, positivity, and the ability to deal with challenges and difficult situations. Let's discuss these one at a time.

Preparation

Preparing well is probably the most important thing you can do in advance to ensure you realize the full potential of your experience abroad. The more you learn about your host country, the better. Of course, luck plays a part as well, but people who prepare seem to have more "luck" than others. "Luck," said the Roman philosopher Seneca, "is when preparation meets opportunity." Spend time on preparation.

Attitude

A French writer once said, "We do not see things as they are, but as we are." Our attitudes control more than we realize. If you are tolerant, you will easily thrive in your new home. In some parts of sub-Saharan Africa, there is a time concept known as "African Time." Buses leave not according to a schedule, but when they are filled up. Shops close not according to stated closing hours, but when the owner feels it's time to close. Meetings start not necessarily at the agreed-upon time, but when everyone has shown up. Now, depending upon where you are from, this may seem either ridiculous or completely normal. However, this way of functioning is neither better nor worse than what you are used to; it is just different. Do not close your mind and accept only what you're used to at home. Accepting cultural differences will help you have a more positive experience abroad.

Observation

It is easy to feel insecure when you move into a new home, start at a new school, and are confronted daily by a new culture. How are you supposed to act? What are the unwritten rules? Some insecurity is inevitable, and it is this insecurity that so often leads to cultural misunderstandings. But if you are observant, it will be easier to avoid these misunderstandings and become integrated into the culture. Watch how those around you are acting. Try to notice the small things. How do the students at school interact with teachers? How do the teachers respond when students have not done their homework or interrupt the class? What rules are important for your host family? If it is important to them that you say where you're going when you leave the house, you should make an extra effort to do so. If it is important for one of your host siblings to watch his or her favorite television program every day after school, you should give up the TV if you're using it. Watch how the people around you interact with each other in general. By being observant, you can learn quite a bit while becoming a part of the community.

Communication

Nobody can tell what you're thinking, what you don't understand, or what you're wondering about. Communication is important because it eliminates uncertainty and makes interacting with other people easier. Especially with your host family and at school, communication will be key to resolving many of the problems that may arise during your stay abroad. If there is anything you do not understand or do not know how to do, talk to those who are around you so that you can avoid any confusion.

Consider the following example:

You get a ride to school with your host mother every morning. She has asked you to be ready every morning at 8:15 a.m. Unfortunately, there is only one bathroom available to you and your entire host family. This slight inconvenience makes you five minutes late every morning. Your host mother doesn't understand why you are always running late, and she feels that you are taking advantage of her generosity in taking you to school. It bothers you to be five minutes late every morning since you are a very punctual person, but the problem seems quite apparent to you, so you don't think to mention it to anyone. Finally one morning, your host mother becomes frustrated and screams at you for being, yet again, five minutes late.

Situations like this often can be avoided with very simple communication. It is impossible for you to know what anyone else is thinking if you don't ask, and no one else can read your mind, either. It is important to realize that good communication solves most problems—and great communication prevents problems from arising in the first place.

Real-life experience
The main thing I learned was that we absolutely *must* communicate with our host family and friends. This way we not only learn a lot about the other culture, but also much about ourselves and our own prejudices.
—former exchange student to Texas, USA

Travel advice
Do not criticize, complain, or condemn. It's okay to say that you are used to doing something a certain way, but do not turn it into criticism of others' way of doing it. That merely creates hard feelings and unnecessary tension.

Interest

Show interest in the people around you. Try to engage in the activities that are important to your host family. Even if you're not a fan of their activities, doing things together with your host family is a really good way to build a strong relationship with them.

Positivity

Try to be positive and look at the bright side of any situation. Smile and be happy! If you are a positive person, it gives others a better impression of you and makes it easier for others to approach you and build a relationship with you. Research has also shown that staying positive will make you enjoy life more—and even live longer!

Dealing with Challenges, Difficult Situations, and Misunderstandings

Almost all exchange students will face challenges and difficult situations during the year. If these situations are handled properly, their negative effects will be minimized. If you suspect that you have acted in a manner that might be considered rude or inappropriate in the host culture, you should always talk to those involved to see how you can avoid any negative consequences.

Travel advice

When *cultural* misunderstandings occur, be humble, but make sure to emphasize that you are used to a different way of doing things and that there has been a misunderstanding. It is not always easy for the host family, teachers, or others to see that there has been a misunderstanding. Then apologize for the incident and ask if there is anything you can do to make up for it.

Other Tips for a Successful Year

- Do not use every opportunity to talk about how everything is better at home. You will only seem self-righteous, and no one likes that.
- Exchange contact information with other exchange students. They can be good to talk to if things don't go so well since they're experiencing much of the same as you.
- Maintain a good relationship with your contact person. It will be invaluable if or when you face difficulties during your stay.
- If you have younger siblings in your host family, play with them. This is a great way to become integrated into the family while learning the language and culture.

Chapter 14

Host Family

Most exchange programs involve staying with a host family. The family is the core of any culture and also gives your stay abroad a safe home base. Staying with a host family is also a great opportunity to learn and experience a lot that would otherwise be difficult. In addition, you get the chance to form close ties to people from another culture. Many exchange students keep in contact with their host families for many years after they go back home, and some maintain contact for a lifetime. Student exchange without a host family would simply not be the same.

What Characterizes a Typical Host Family?

This is a difficult question to answer since no family is the same. A host family could have one child, several children, grown children, or no children at all. The host family might live in a very large city or in a very small community in the countryside. Some families have hosted exchange students in the past, and some have not. It is not uncommon for host families to have children who either are or have been exchange students. The host family also could have more than one exchange student staying with them at the same time. And it's possible that the host family consists of only one person or one parent with children.

Ultimately, the number of people in the host family isn't really important. Neither is where they live or what kind of cars they drive. The host family has been selected because they want to have an exchange student living with them, and because they want to share their culture and their way of life with others. This is reflected in the fact that host families usually don't get paid to have an exchange student living with them. Even if they are paid something, it's usually not enough to cover the expenses associated with having an extra member in the family.

Fun fact—Did you know that . . .
in Russia, Christmas is celebrated on the January 7 instead of December 24/25?

What Kind of Host Family Is the Best for Me?

There is no rule to determine what type of host family is best to live with. A host family that has had several exchange students in the past may have valuable experience that will benefit you. But their previous experience can also raise their expectations of you and perhaps diminish their enthusiasm for showing you around and entertaining you. A host family with children can provide you with a new brother or sister who can offer great support throughout the year, while a family without children may have more time for you.

So come to peace with the host family that you get. Do not waste time on speculation or disappointment. As it has been said before, the success of your exchange year lies mostly on your shoulders anyway, so you need to keep an open attitude.

Fun fact—Did you know that . . .
in Japan, people sleep on thin mattresses on the
floor called *futons*?

Your First Days with Your New Host Family

It is common for your host family to be extra nice to you
during your first few days with them. Because you are new
to the family, they'll want to give you a warm welcome and
take special care of you. Expect to be treated more like a guest
than as a family member during your first few weeks there.
Sooner or later, however, everyday life with school and other
activities will set in, and you should expect to become just a
normal member of the family. But don't forget to enjoy the
first days!

Real-life experience
There is some slang in New Zealand that took time
to understand! The first day I arrived in my new
home and met my host family, they said: "It's tea in
fifteen minutes." I thought that we were drinking
tea in fifteen minutes, which was not so strange. But
we never had any tea. So I thought maybe they just
forgot about it . . . and then we ate dinner. The next
day before I was in school, they said, "Remember
we are going to have tea about five o'clock." So I
thought I had come to an old-fashioned family
who wanted me to come home to drink tea at five?!
But it turned out that *tea* meant "dinner," which
explained a whole lot!
—former exchange student to New Zealand

A Different Family

As an exchange student living with a new family, you will experience a number of differences from your own family that you have to adapt to or at least get used to. Some of these differences will be cultural, while other differences will depend on your particular family. How the home of your host family is furnished, what type of food they eat, their rules, and what they expect of you are probably based on both culture and on their particular preferences and beliefs.

It is impossible to say exactly what will be different and what you will have to get used to, except that it will be a lot. So stay open to these new situations and try to not make things more difficult than they already are.

Remember that what you experience as different, for whatever reason, is not better or worse than what you're used to; it is simply different. There is not one right answer to when a family should eat dinner, how often a family should clean their house, or how many TVs a family should own.

Your Role in the Family

Some exchange students feel confused about their role in the host family. They have paid a lot to travel, so why should they also help clean the dishes? It is often said that an exchange student is neither an au pair (someone who is there to help around the house) nor a houseguest (someone who is there to do anything *but* help around the house). Exchange students fit into a category of their own. The general rule: you are part of the family and therefore must help the family with their daily chores, just as anyone else in the family would. What this means and how much you have to help will vary greatly from host family to host family, just as it does at home. Your responsibilities may be to walk the dog in the morning, clean out the dishwasher, and pick up your new host brother or sister from football practice.

In some parts of the world, it is common to have a maid who does the family's housework. Students who come from such a family will likely have to do more housework while on exchange than they're used to doing at home.

Family Rules and Routines

Because family rules and routines are rarely written down, you will have to learn to pick up little clues as time goes by. However, there are some common routines and tasks that you should ask your host family about. We have made this list:

Rules and Routines to Ask Your Host Family

- your responsibility for household chores
- the procedure for washing clothes
- rules for showering and use of the bathroom in the morning
- safety precautions
- transportation arrangements when going out or to school
- storage for your toiletries and personal belongings
- mealtimes and meal procedures
- school lunch arrangements
- your bedtime and curfew
- rules for visiting friends and having friends over
- rules for using the family's telephone, computer, and Internet
- rules for using the stereo, TV, and other electronics

Travel advice

Talk to your host family during one of the first days about their rules and routines, what they expect of you, and how they want you to help around the house.

Host Family Member

Although you will become a new member of your host family, you will still have your real family back home. Also, the other members of your host family know each other better than you know them. This is no surprise since they have lived together for years. These two facts constitute a small but important distinction in your relationship with the others in your host family. It is what we can call the "1 percent difference." This difference can sometimes make it difficult to know exactly how to behave or respond in certain situations. Sometimes, you will find it hard to act as you would with your own family and to be 100 percent yourself. At home with your own family, you can break the rules, shout, or do other unacceptable things because you are confident in your relationship with your parents. Your parents know you very well. They know how to react if you behave unacceptably, and you know what to expect.

But with your host family, shouting, screaming, or other "special behavior" can cause a lot of uncertainty on their part. They simply do not know you well enough to feel secure about how to react. Because of this small difference, a lot of exchange students find it difficult to argue with their host parents. "At home I would not have been afraid to shout or nag until I got things my way," one exchange student admitted. "But with my host parents, I can't do that."

Being an exchange student sometimes means having to put aside your own pride and stubbornness and accept being yourself only 99 percent.

This 1 percent difference also applies to your host parents. After all, they are not your legal parents. They will sometimes feel that they cannot treat you exactly as they treat their own children.

What Should I Call My Host Parents?

Some exchange students call their host parents Mom and Dad, while others use only their first (given) names. Some also call them Aunt or Uncle, or use their last name. It's most common to use their first names. But what is natural for you will depend on what is common in the host country and what your host parents prefer you to call them. It is probably best to simply to ask them: "What would you like me to call you?" By doing this, you will erase any awkwardness that could arise when you need to address your host parents.

What Do I Pay For, and What Does the Host Family Pay For?

As an exchange student, you will live and eat for free. But you should expect to use your own pocket money for activities that don't involve the family. Some typical examples are mobile phone use, bus fare, food you eat outside the home, travels done without the host family, etc. When it comes to activities that you do together with the host family that cost money, who pays depends on the nature of the activity. Often it will be clear to you. Some host families will offer to pay for things exchange students are supposed to cover themselves, but this is not something you can assume that your host family will do.

A special case is expensive travel. Imagine that your host family had planned an expensive vacation before they decided to host you, and that you can't afford to pay for it yourself. Should the host family pay your way? Many exchange organizations have a principle that if the host family is unable to pay for the exchange student while on vacation, the exchange student will be given the opportunity to live somewhere else in the meantime, for example with acquaintances of the host family or with the contact person.

Travel advice
If you are unsure if you should pay for something—ask!

Should I Adapt to My Host Family, or Should They Adapt to Me?

For the most part, you should be the one adapting to your host family, not the other way around. That's what student exchange is all about—adapting to new cultures! This does not mean that the host family should not or will not pay attention to your needs. Hopefully, they will to some degree try to adapt to you, too. But remember that it is you who have come to their home and to their home country!

Host Siblings

It is hard to know in advance how your host siblings will feel about getting a new "brother" or "sister." Maybe they are looking forward to getting a new sibling with whom they can share experiences. But it may also be that they don't have much time to spare, or that they do not wish to have a close relationship with a new exchange student. The best thing you can do is to just see how things play out and to not have too high expectations.

Even if you have host brothers and sisters who are your own age and introduce you to their circle of friends, you should still try to find your own friends after a while. It is not healthy in the long run to rely on your host siblings every time you want to hang out with other people.

You should also be aware that it is not uncommon for host siblings to become a bit jealous of their new brother or sister. All of a sudden, they have to share everything with you (parents, grandparents, friends, TVs, bikes, etc.), and they might feel that you're receiving some kind of special treatment from their parents.

If you do not get along so well with one of your siblings, try to improve the relationship by taking the initiative to find something you both like to do. For example, playing a game of basketball or cooking a meal together. If you are trying your best to develop a new relationship but your host sibling does not seem interested, don't get upset. You do not need to be best friends! Maybe he or she simply does not want to enter into a close relationship with an exchange student.

Travel advice
Problems with host siblings? Talk with your host parents about it.

How to Ensure a Good Relationship with the Host Family

Ensuring a good relationship with your host family is a mutual responsibility, but as the exchange student, you are expected to make the biggest changes. The principles that apply to building and maintaining a good relationship with your host family are the same as the general principles presented in chapter 13, with one important addition: gratitude. Your host family opens up their home to you for an entire year, and you need to show that you do not take their hospitality for granted. Make dinner for your host family, buy a bouquet of flowers for your host mother, invite the family out for ice cream, or find something else nice to do during the exchange year. It doesn't need to be expensive or complicated; it's the thought that counts. Random acts of kindness go a long way!

Chapter 15

School

As an exchange student, you will spend a lot of your time at school. School is where you will sharpen your knowledge of the host country's language, and it is where much of your learning will take place. But school is also much more than that. It's the place where you'll get to know new people and make many new friends. It's where you'll share laughs and experiences with others. School is an important part of student exchange, and it is where many of the memories from the exchange year are created.

Student Role

As an exchange student, you will take part in school on an equal basis with other students. You will be formally registered as a student there, and the same rules and expectations that apply to everyone else will also apply to you.

On the other hand, you do not have the same academic foundation as your peers. You do not speak the host country's language as well as they do, and you do not have the same educational background. In addition, you will be a student at the school for only a limited amount of time, and you are not depending on graduating from that school.

Going to School Abroad

Until now, you have known what is expected of you as a student—the written and unwritten rules regarding homework, being tardy, talking in class, etc. You know how much you have to study to pass a test, and you know how to write an essay. Although some of these rules will be the same in your new country, many of them may be different, and you need to prepare yourself for an abrupt change in your schooling.

As an exchange student, you will have to relearn many of the dynamics that are second nature to you at home. Each country has its own set of rules for how things work in schools. The school itself may be stricter or more easygoing than what you're used to.

In Norway, for example, schools are known for being very easygoing. Students address teachers by their first names, and teachers don't punish students for not having done their homework. This is because education is seen as the student's own responsibility, not the teacher's to force upon the students. In addition, teachers cannot give students detention, and students can skip classes without permission from their teacher or school. This is in contrast to many countries, such as the United States. At many schools in the USA, showing up to class thirty seconds late several times may result in a detention. A student who continues to be tardy may have to come to school on a Saturday to serve detention or, even worse, could be suspended from school for a period of time.

The point here is not that being tardy is seen as very serious in the USA and not in Norway, but that every country has its own way to run a school. There is no right way or wrong way to do it; there are just different ways. As an exchange student you will experience a different way of going to school. These new experiences will contribute to making your year abroad more interesting.

Real-life experience
Something that was new to me was the school
uniform, which I had only encountered in movies. It
was a fun experience having to use a school uniform,
and I became a pro at tying a tie—something that
actually came in handy later!
        —former exchange student to New Zealand

What Is Required of Me
as a Foreign Exchange Student?

When you choose to sign up for a school year abroad, you will
be expected to take school just as seriously as you take it at
home, if not more seriously. This means going to school every
day, doing your homework, showing up for class on time, and
refraining from talking or sleeping in class.

You may worry that your new school will expect you to
make good grades. But that might be hard, especially because
of your limited language skills. The important thing is not
what grades you get, but the effort that you show. Doing your
best is far more important than getting good grades. Teachers
will understand that you cannot perform as well your native
peers, but they will not have sympathy for laziness or
disruptive behavior.

Why Is It So Important to Make an Effort at School?

Showing up late, sleeping in class, being noisy, skipping
homework, exerting minimal effort, or otherwise becoming
the teacher's enemy is never a good idea, and doing so as an
exchange student can be catastrophic. Why? As an exchange
student, you are a guest. You are not entitled to education
in the same way that your peers are. That means you can be

thrown out of school at any time and sent straight back home. In the school's eyes, you are a visiting student who is there to learn. So if you are disrupting the education of other students, why should the school keep you?

If you get kicked out of school, you can expect the exchange organization to remove you from its program and send you home. Your exchange year is first and foremost a "school year abroad," and if you can't meet the minimum expectations for a student, you have little right to be in school. Therefore, be on your best behavior at all times. Although very few students get sent back to their home country, it does happen from time to time, and you should always take this into consideration when you are doing anything that could be seen as negative. Making a good impression at school will also be very valuable should you run into serious trouble with your host family.

Travel advice
Make an effort in school. Make sure the school and your teachers get a good impression of you. A good reputation ensures that you will have a successful time as a student and also makes each school day more enjoyable. In addition, it will be helpful if you ever face problems with your host family.

What Grade Should I Be In?

If your host school is unsure about what grade level (eleventh, twelfth, etc.) is right for you, you may get to take part in the decision. Usually, it is best to select a grade with the level of difficulty similar to what you would have experienced had you stayed at home. However, if you speak very little of the host country's language, learning the language properly will be a great challenge to you. In that case, if you can chose between two grades, it may be wise to choose the lower grade. Being one year older (or younger) than your classmates is no big deal. If you are really unsure, it may be wise to start at the higher grade, and then go down one grade if you feel the coursework and language barrier are too difficult. It is often easier to go down a grade than the other way around.

Real-life experience
I started in the twelfth grade with people my own age but switched after three months to eleventh grade. I understood more of what the teachers said, and the classes became more interesting and fun.
—former exchange student to Germany

What Subjects Should I Choose?

You will not find a school abroad that offers the exact same classes as your school at home, but your new school may offer similar classes. In addition, schools abroad often offer courses that your school at home does not have. If you need to get the exchange year approved as part of your high school education at home, take this into account when selecting courses. Try to choose class subjects that are similar to the ones you will be missing out on at home. If you do not need to get the exchange year approved, you are free to choose whatever courses interest you the most.

Travel advice
If your exchange year does not replace a grade in school in your home country, choose exciting and fun subjects that you do not have at home.

Graduation, Transcripts, and Diplomas

Most likely, you will be graded just like your fellow students. However, getting good grades will not be as important for you as it will be for your peers. If you need to get the exchange year approved by your home school, you'll most likely be required just to pass all your classes, not achieve a certain grade point average.

At the end of your exchange year, you'll probably receive some sort of diploma or certificate to show that you studied at the school. If you don't receive this automatically, you should request it. You never know when you may need it, and it may be good to have for job or university applications later.

If you are a last-year student, you may even have the opportunity to graduate and get a foreign high school diploma. In that case, you may have to provide your host school with transcripts or other proof of prior education. If you get this opportunity, don't let it pass you by. Having a foreign high school diploma is invaluable and will do a lot more for you than you think.

Chapter 16

New Friends

A school year abroad gives you a great opportunity to establish new friendships with people from other countries. School provides a natural setting for getting to know many new people who may become lifelong friends. You'll probably get to know other exchange students as well, so by the end of the year, you may have friends from all over the world!

Finding New Friends as an Exchange Student

Some exchange students worry that they won't be able to find new friends abroad because the people they meet will already have "enough" friends. Fortunately, this is very rarely true. It can actually be easier to find new friends as an exchange student. As an exchange student, you will be a very interesting person to many people.

Making friends may take a little longer for some exchange students than for others, but they all make friends eventually. A few exchange students are able to make plans for the afternoon with new friends on the first day of school, but most need a little more time. Do not be discouraged if you haven't made any friends after the first few weeks. That's completely normal. But make sure not to give up!

Real-life experience
At the beginning of the stay, there were so many people who were interested in me. I was an interesting person who came from an unknown country. But eventually I was not so exciting for them anymore, and I started to feel a little lonely. Fortunately, I learned that friendship is created over time, and after a while I got more friends who called me and who I could call to hang out.

—former exchange student to Wisconsin, USA

When you are trying to make new friends, it is a good idea to participate in sports or other group activities. Regular group activities represent an optimal setting for meeting new people and developing friendships.

Travel advice
Participate in as many activities as possible.

Remember that being outgoing helps a lot. You cannot always expect other people to be the ones to talk to you first. More important, you have very little to lose by going over to anyone and initiating a conversation. The worst that can happen is that he or she will not want to talk to you—and that is his or her loss, not yours.

Real-life experience
I joined the ski team and the soccer team and got my best friends throughout the year from these clubs.

—former exchange student
to New Hampshire, USA

The principles for a successful exchange year, discussed in chapter 13, also apply to finding new friends in your host country.

Other Exchange Students

It is not uncommon for several exchange students to attend the same school. You also may have met other exchange students during the program's orientations or meetings. Exchange students are all in the same boat, and they often get along well. Because of this unifying bond, other exchange students, especially those from your own country, offer tremendous support because they are going through much of the same experiences as you are.

However, you should not spend all of your time with other exchange students. If you do, you won't become well integrated into the new culture, and you will miss out on a lot of the experiences associated with an exchange year. This is especially true if you just hang out with other exchange students from your own country. This can be destructive and it is against the purpose of an exchange year. In addition, you won't become particularly good in the language of your host country. This is the main reason why exchange organizations rarely place two exchange students from the same country in the same host family.

The Meaning of *Friend* and *Friendship* Abroad

What is the difference between a friend and an acquaintance? How well do you have to know someone before you become friends? This is a tough question to answer. In fact, there really is no answer; the meaning of the word *friend* varies from country to country. In the USA, the term is used for almost all acquaintances, while in Russia it is used only for a few people who are very close.

It's good to be aware that the meaning you put into the word *friend* may not necessarily be the same as what others put into it.

Travel advice
If you are invited to do something, say *yes* even if you're not overly enthusiastic about the invitation (assuming that the invitation is not unpleasant). A *no* can be taken personally, and you may not be invited to do anything again.

Chapter 17

Homesickness and Other Challenges

No two days are ever the same, and as an exchange student you will probably run into challenges now and again. Homesickness may be such a challenge. Even though challenges can be unpleasant at the time, they do actually help you become a wiser and more independent person. It may be good to remember this when times are tough.

Homesickness

When you miss the people you love and the life you are used to, it is easy to feel a bit down and unmotivated. Occasional homesickness is a natural part of living far from home for a long period of time. Some people hardly ever experience it, while others can get it more often. It's not unusual to feel homesick just after arriving in the host country, during holidays, days off, and birthdays. Hearing news of negative events in the home country or just feeling down or tired for some other reason may also trigger homesickness.

Keep in mind that homesickness is all in your head, and fortunately it passes. There are a number of ways to fight homesickness and it's up to you to find out which one works best for you. The worst thing you can do is to feel sorry for yourself, as this will only make things worse.

The first thing that many people want to do when they feel homesick is to telephone home. Many student exchange organizations advise against this, as it can make you feel even more homesick.

Advice for Dealing with Homesickness

- Go have some fun! Hang out with friends to get your mind off your homesickness and cheer yourself up.
- If you can't find anything fun to do with your friends, try cleaning up your room or taking a walk around the neighborhood—anything to stay busy.
- Try to improve your mood by thinking about all the positive things you have experienced.
- Talk to someone who understands you, for example another exchange student or someone in your host family.
- Make an entry in your diary to express your frustrations and feelings.
- Try not to think so much about life back home and the people you miss. Doing this will only increase your homesickness.
- Do not do any wishful thinking, for example wishing you were going home in the morning.
- Talk to your contact person about your homesickness.
- Write a letter or an e-mail and send it the next day after rereading it.

Preventing Homesickness

Although there's no guarantee against homesickness, there are some things you can do to minimize the chance of getting it. Try some of these tips:

- Try filling your time with useful activities. Play team sports or engage in other regular activities.
- Communicate with your family and friends at home by e-mail or letter.
- Limit your phone calls back home. Make appointments before calling.
- Limit the time you spend chatting on the phone or on Facebook with those back home.
- Get familiar with your new environment and those around you. Make a regular effort to integrate yourself.
- Write down a list of all the things you get to participate in or be a part of as an exchange student.

By staying active and building up your sense of belonging to your new community, you won't have time to get homesick. This is the very best way to avoid homesickness in the first place.

If you experience homesickness that lasts several weeks or months and you feel very depressed, perhaps you should consider dropping out of the program. You might not have been away from home before, and maybe it's too soon for you to live a year abroad. There is no shame in going back home again. Perhaps you will be more prepared for such an experience at a later point in your life!

Language Difficulties and Frustration

Learning a whole new language from the ground up and knowing it well takes time. If you experience daily challenges because you can't manage the language well, there's only one thing to do: work harder to learn it, and *practice*!

See suggestions about language training in chapter 8. If your host family has small children, they are great for practicing simple conversations in your host country's language.

Culture Shock

Culture shock happens when the new culture is so strange and confusing that it becomes difficult to adapt to and you don't know how to manage your emotions. If this happens to you, don't be discouraged; culture shock is generally short-lived. Besides, you are not alone: anyone who travels to a foreign country can experience this feeling. There are a few things you can do to reduce or even prevent culture shock, like reading about the host country's culture ahead of time and talking with others who understand it well. It can also be helpful to discuss your feelings with other exchange students.

School Challenges

If you find it hard to keep up with your schoolwork, it could be that you don't understand the language well enough, or you may have been placed in a grade level that is too high for you. In either case, you should ask your teachers if you can be moved down a grade.

Sometimes you can ask the school to make special arrangements for you, such as offering certain classes at a lower level or giving you more time for independent study. Ultimately, though, it is the school's decision. Some schools will insist that you take classes at the same level as all the other students your age, even though you are a visiting student. Other schools might be more flexible and customize a special program for you.

If you have other problems at school, discuss them with your host family, contact person, or school advisor. They are all there to help you, so make use of them if you need help.

Host Family Challenges

No family is perfect, not even host families. There is no such thing as the perfect exchange student, either. Misunderstandings, minor disagreements, and stressful days occur in any host family, just as they do with your family back home. This doesn't necessarily mean the host family is bad—it just confirms that no family is perfect.

However, if your relationship with your host family is clearly bad, then something must be done about it. In such a case, it's important that you and the host family get to the bottom of any problems and try to resolve them together. Talk with your host family about what you feel isn't working and listen to what they have to say. Ask whether you are at fault and what you can do to help make things work better. A good, long chat with your host family is often enough to restore a good relationship and get things back on track again.

If this does not resolve things, you can request a change to a different host family. Before you do this, however, it is vital that you try to resolve the problems yourself. In fact, it is more difficult to change your host family without first having done this.

Difficult Choices

As an exchange student, as in all aspects of your life, you will frequently have to make difficult decisions. For example, you will have signed a contract prior to your departure agreeing to abide by certain rules, but sometimes it might be very tempting to break them. Almost every exchange program forbids exchange students from drinking alcohol. There are many good reasons for this. But imagine that you are at a party with some friends and spirits are running high. You have an urge to drink. Will you?

One should not break the rules that govern student exchanges. Yet, some students choose to do so. Regardless, it is important to consider the potential consequences breaking the rules can have. For example, if you stay in the USA, where the minimum age for alcohol consumption and possession is typically twenty-one, getting caught drinking or possessing alcohol could be very troublesome—you would be breaking the law. The consequences would also depend on your host family's attitude toward your actions.

Obviously, you risk being sent back home if your American host family has to pick you up drunk from a police station, especially after you had been asked not to drink in the first place. Even if you are legally able to drink in your own country, you should think twice before drinking while you are an exchange student.

Ending the School Year Early

Every year, a small number of exchange students choose to return home early. There are various reasons for this—unrealistic expectations, bad luck, homesickness, illness, troubles with the host family or finding new friends, the death or illness of a family member back home, or just general dissatisfaction with the entire experience.

If you find yourself considering ending the school year early and returning home, talk with someone first. Speak with your contact person, your host family, or your family back home. Think it over carefully. Maybe something can be done to improve things so that you don't have to end up leaving. However, if you do decide to return home, just be at peace with your decision. Even if it's the right thing for you to do, you've still had many valuable experiences.

Real-life experience

I had been in the USA for four months when I chose to return home. There were several reasons for this. I had changed host families, but I wasn't satisfied with the new one, either. Additionally, I had stomach problems. It was embarrassing for friends and family to have me return home so soon, and it bothered me for a long time. Looking back, however, I learned to view it in a much more positive way. I realized how much I had learned in those four months—especially about myself, about how much I had grown in that half year, and how much I had experienced. I concluded that I had no regret about going to the USA, nor that I had ended my stay there earlier than originally planned.

—former exchange student to Minnesota, USA.

Chapter 18

Change of Host Family

Sometimes the relationship between the exchange student and his or her host family does not work out well. In such instances, the student may request a change of host families, but it is then important to proceed properly.

When Can I Change My Host Family?

A change of host family can usually only take place after you have tried to resolve your issues with your family without any positive results. This process is important, because trying to solve problems with your host family on your own often leads to a better relationship between you and your host family. This will eliminate the need to change families. Also, if you talk to your host family on your own, the exchange organization will know that you really tried to make things work. If you don't bother to try to solve your problems with your family, how can the organization know that things will be more successful with a new one?

As a rule of thumb, if the relationship with your host family does not improve after several attempts to improve it, and the chemistry is simply not right, you may change your host family.

The problem between you and your host family must be something so fundamental that it does not allow for peaceful coexistence. Poor reasons for wanting to change families include refusing to adapt to anything new, or feeling that the family is stupid. These are not considered valid reasons to change host families. Here are some other unacceptable reasons for requesting a new host family:

Non-Arguments for Changing Host Families

- Your host family doesn't have cable TV.
- You must wake up earlier than you're used to.
- You have to prepare your own lunch.
- You have to share a room with someone.
- The host family lives too far away from the nearest shopping mall.
- The host family's house is too small.
- The host family does not have Internet.
- You have to help wash dishes after dinner.
- You are not allowed to attend certain parties.
- The host family is religious.
- You cannot play music after ten o'clock in the evening.
- There is only one television, and the host family only watches boring shows.
- The host family listens to classical music.
- You are not allowed to go out of the house after nine on weekdays.
- The host family does not give you pocket money.
- You're used to a higher standard of living than the host family can provide.

If you use arguments like these, you show that you don't understand the purpose of an exchange program. It shows little willingness on your part to adapt to a new way of living. Chances are that if you switch host families for any of these reasons, you will find something similar to be unhappy about in your new family. The real problem here is you—and the exchange organization will know that, too.

Arguments for Changing Host Families

In this chapter, we exclude extreme cases, such as the host family being exploitative (like having you do unreasonable amounts of housework), becoming violent toward you, stealing from you, demanding payment for meals, bullying or harassing you, or locking you out of the house. In such cases, you have to call your exchange organization immediately!

If you feel that you want to change families, it is usually because you find your relationship with the host family very exhausting. This may simply be due to the fact that you and your host family are a bad match and/or you and your family do not feel comfortable living with one another. You may feel that you are not accepted for whom you are, and your host family may feel unappreciated and unaccepted, as well. All these feelings suggest that the situation is nobody's fault—it is simply bad chemistry. If so, there will be good reasons for changing host families. However, your host family may not always share your perception of the situation. If this is the case, it can be hard for your contact person, who receives two different versions of the situation: yours and your host family's. The way you proceed to change host families is therefore very important.

How You Should Proceed

- **Think it over carefully.**
Is it really necessary to change host families? Are there really deep differences between you and your family, or are you just looking for a perfect family that doesn't really exist? Can you be sure that you will be happier with another host family? There may not be a family nearby that can host you, so the possibility of having to change schools or perhaps even move to another part of the country is a definite possibility.

- **Look at yourself.**

See if your behavior may be causing some of the problems. Have you really done your best to adapt? Are you showing interest in your host family, or are you spending most of your time up in your room in front of your computer or reading books in your native language? Do you help your family when they ask for it? Do you have talks with your host family, or do you kill any attempts to have a conversation with short "yes," "no," or "I don't know" answers? Are you never on time for dinner or always coming home late? Do you tell your host parents where you go when you leave the house, and do you ask for permission before using your host father's bike? Do you say thank you and apologize when it is appropriate? By thinking about your own behavior, you might find that you could do a lot to improve the situation. This may be enough to resolve the issues and establish a good relationship.

- **Try to resolve the problems first.**

This is important because it will be difficult to request a change without first having tried to solve the problems on your own. Reassignment will always be the last solution to any problem you have with your host family. So talk to your contact person about the difficulties you are having with your host family and ask for advice, but do not mention anything about changing your host family at this point in time. If you have a sit-down talk with your host family, you can probably solve most of the problems at hand. Remember that good communication is key in these situations. Take special care to voice your opinions respectfully so that your feelings are not misconstrued.

- **Give it a little extra time and effort.**

Rome was not built in a day, and it also takes time to build a good relationship. Make a special effort to make this work. Be extra nice and helpful. Make sure you do what you are asked to do and talk to your family immediately if misunderstandings arise. Keep your room tidy and do not be late for family events like meals. Show that you are really trying. Your contact person should know about the situation and that you are really trying to make things work. Maybe the problems will disappear, and you'll create a really nice relationship with your host family.

- **If nothing improves** . . .
If nothing helps and the situation does not improve, you should prepare to ask for a change of host families. Write a list of reasons why the relationship does not seem to be working and why you want to change. The first thing your contact person will ask you about is why you want to change, so you should have thought out a good answer ahead of time.

- **Talk with your contact person and request a change.**
Tell your contact person about your unsuccessful attempts to improve the situation and that you want to change your host family. It is very important that she or he knows that you have tried to solve the problems and make things work. Explain that you have been thinking the situation over carefully for some time. Do not try to portray your host family as bad people; instead, emphasize that it is the chemistry that is not right. Remember to avoid reasons that will not get any sympathy from your contact person, such as the non-arguments listed earlier in this chapter.

Travel advice
When you want to change your host family, the way you proceed is very important. Before asking for a new family, show that you have really tried to make things work.

> **Travel advice**
> When talking to your contact person about your problems, make sure you are somewhere where you won't be heard or interrupted.

Do Not Do This!

Do not tell your host family that you want to change before you talk to your contact person. You won't gain anything by doing this and it will only make things worse. In addition, if your contact person wants you to try a bit more, you will have put yourself in a very awkward situation. Make sure to stay quiet about these thoughts and remain respectful to your host family.

> **Travel advice**
> Do not threaten your host family that you want to change.

Special Circumstances

Sometimes the contact person is one of the host family's friends, acquaintances, or work colleagues, or the host mother or father is a contact person for other exchange students. If this is the case, you must be very careful when you explain why you want to change host families. It is extremely important that you emphasize that you simply do not fit together, and that you disagree on some fundamental things that cannot be worked out. Do not portray your host family as difficult or bad people.

Another special case is if you have already changed your host family once. Unfortunately for you, it can easily look as though you are the problem since you want to change your host family yet again. You'll need to pay special attention to how you approach your discussions with your contact person so that you don't look like you are the root of all the problems.

Travel advice

When requesting a change in host families, be extra careful about how you proceed if . . .

- the contact person is one of your host family's good friends.
- one of your host parents is a contact person for other exchange students.
- you've already changed your host family before.

In these special cases, it is more important than anything else that you proceed in a positive manner. Always emphasize that there is some basic problem between you and your host family that cannot be resolved, no matter how hard you try. You might also want to contact the main office of your exchange organization in your host country and talk to someone there. Remember to explain why this is a special circumstance.

If Your Request Is Denied

If you are not allowed to change host families, it is most likely because your contact person believes that the problems you have with the host family are not such that changing families is the right solution. If you strongly disagree, discuss your situation with another contact person (if you have one) or with the main office of your exchange organization in your host country. Sometimes a student is in a situation where a change is desirable, but finding a new host family is difficult. Some exchange students have then experienced that changing host families may be easier if they know a family who can host them.

If Your Request Is Accepted

There is always extra work for your exchange organization when you change host families. First, your contact person must find a new host family, which then must be approved. This may take some time, so you need to be understanding of that. If the problems between you and your host family are very severe, you may be given the option of staying temporarily with another family or your contact person. Sometimes exchange students know other families that are willing to host them. This can make the process go more quickly.

Leaving Your Original Host Family

No matter how much time you have left with your original host family, try to make that time as comfortable as possible for everyone involved. No one will benefit if your last days are unpleasant, and you don't want your last memories of your old host family to be disagreeable. Do not forget that your host family tried their best, and the situation certainly has not been easy for them, either. When you leave, consider thanking your host family for having welcomed you into their home and express your sorrow that it did not work out as you had hoped.

When you arrive at the home of your new host family, you'll have a brand-new start. You will have grown and matured from your previous experiences, and now you'll have the chance to build a good relationship from scratch. Use this opportunity wisely, and remember the importance of communication when building a new relationship!

Chapter 19

The Final Weeks and the Travel Back Home

By now, you have probably reached the stage where you know both your host country's language and culture very well. You have made many good friends and have become used to your new life there. On the one hand, you may wish you could stay in your host country longer. On the other hand, you are probably looking forward to seeing everyone at home again. The last weeks as an exchange student are often filled with many mixed emotions. These last few weeks will greatly influence how you will look back on your exchange year, and a good ending will help cap off a successful year abroad.

Behave

Have you been good throughout the year; do not break the rules now! It's easy to think that it does not matter what you do since you are going home soon. But there's no reason to risk ruining a nice finish to your year by being sent home early.

The Last Few Weeks

There are usually many things you'll need to take care of before you can leave the home where you have lived for almost a year. Take care of them well in advance so you won't have to worry about them during your last few days. If you have a lot to do, you may want to set up a plan so that you do not become stressed and cranky. Planning ahead always helps you avoid last-minute problems.

Travel advice
Think about everything you must do before going home, and do as much of it as early as possible. That way you will avoid last-minute stress and use your last few days as an exchange student to do something nice and relaxing.

Packing

Check with your airline to review the luggage policy for your flight home. Once you know how much you can bring back, try to get an overview of what you want to bring home, what can be thrown away, and what can be given away. If you have made a lot of purchases throughout the year, you will probably have to mail a package home because there won't be enough room in your suitcase for all your new things. Alternatively, if you know you'll be returning soon for a visit, you may politely ask your host family to store some of your things for you.

Overweight luggage can end up being very expensive, and many airlines refuse to carry luggage that weighs more than 32 kg (70 lb.) Therefore, remember to weigh your luggage before you leave to make sure you can bring it on the plane with you.

Travel advice

If you need to mail a package home, examine different alternatives to find the cheapest one. Make sure to do all this research early! Remember to pack everything carefully as packages are often treated roughly. Also, never mail expensive items like jewelry.

Travel advice

If you want to keep your class notes and other school papers, scan them and save them to a memory stick. This will save you room and weight.

Saying Good-Bye

Remember to say good-bye to everyone who has been especially helpful or nice to you, such as your contact person, neighbors, teachers, and other people with whom you have become close over the year. If you're unable to say good-bye in person, call them or send a card, e-mail, or text message. They will undoubtedly appreciate it.

Farewell Gifts

If you have had a very good relationship with your host family, consider giving them a farewell gift as a symbol of your appreciation. It does not need to be anything big or expensive—just something that they will enjoy. If you have had a very helpful contact person, you may also want give him or her a small gift as well. Remember, many contact people work as volunteers, receiving little or no compensation.

Going Away Party

A farewell party is a great way to say good-bye to your friends and other people you have gotten to know during your exchange year. If you can't have a party at your host family's home, see if you can have it at a restaurant or at a friend's home.

Your host family may have planned to do something with you before you leave, such as a nice dinner. Therefore, you should talk to your host family about any plans you make with your friends during your last days.

Your Last Night as an Exchange Student

Before you go to bed, make sure that your bags are properly packed and that you can get into them for the things you will need the next day (toiletries, etc.). Most important, make sure that you have your passport and flight ticket. By now, you should have cleaned your room and checked to see that you haven't left any garbage behind including school papers or magazines. You should leave your room the same or in better condition than it was in when you arrived. Check with your airline to make sure that your flight has not been changed or canceled, and charge your mobile phone.

Checklist

- ☐ Pay back any borrowed money.
- ☐ Return any borrowed items (books, clothes, etc.).
- ☐ Make sure you have all important documents (flight tickets, passport, etc.).
- ☐ Pack your suitcase.
- ☐ Prepare or mail any package (if needed).

- ☐ Do all the little things you've planned to do before leaving (take pictures of your school, host family and friends, buy souvenirs, etc.)
- ☐ Clean your room.
- ☐ Say good-bye and thank people who have helped you through the year.
- ☐ Exchange contact information with anyone you wish to stay in contact with.
- ☐ Purchase a small thank-you gift for your host family.

The Travel Day

Check one last time that you still have your passport and plane tickets, and that you're not leaving anything behind. Saying good-bye at the airport can be very emotional—and there's no shame in shedding some tears. It shows that you've had a good year. As with your trip to your host country, if you have to transfer flights one or more times on the way home, always go straight to the next gate. And remember that your host family will want to hear that you arrived safely, so do not forget to let them know when you are home safe and sound.

Travel advice
Write a farewell letter to your host family (don't forget to thank them) and give it to them at the airport. They will appreciate it.

Congratulations!

Participating in a high school student exchange program is a once-in-a-lifetime opportunity. You have embraced this experience and followed through the entire way. No matter how satisfied or dissatisfied you may be with your experience abroad, you are a much better person now because of it. You've learned a new language and have gotten to know another culture from the inside out. You have had to look after yourself, and the journey has been a transformative experience. You have grown up quite a bit since you were last home! Use what you have learned on what lies ahead of you. Just as you seized this opportunity, seize life—it is waiting for you to take advantage of it!

Chapter 20

Back Home

Twenty-four hours ago, you were living in a foreign country. Now, suddenly, you are back home, where everything seems to be just as it was when you left it. But actually something did change during the year you were gone. It may be hard to detect, but that something is *you*!

A New You

All the experiences, people, and places you've encountered have, without a doubt, changed you forever. You are a slightly different person than you used to be—most likely a better person. All the experience you have gathered from the many new situations you've faced has helped you grow into a more competent person. You are more mature. You have acquired invaluable language skills. You probably have a broader and more balanced world-view. You have learned a lot that others your age do not know. You understand a great deal about one particular culture, which may, in turn, make it easier to understand other cultures. You have certainly changed, but it is not always easy for those around you to notice that you've changed—at least not at first glance.

Readjusting to Life Back Home

It takes time to adapt to a foreign culture, but once you have, that culture becomes part of your daily life, and you may even forget that you're living in a foreign country. However, before you become well integrated, you may feel surprised, culture shocked, or even homesick.

When you have adapted to a new culture and then return home, you go through all these stages all over again. It may actually feel strange to be back at home. All the routines you have become accustomed to over the last year are suddenly replaced by the same old routines from before you left. But now it's those old routines that feel different. They may seem old-fashioned, impractical, or frustrating.

In fact, you may even long to go back to your host country, especially if it was extremely different from your home. This is what is called "reverse culture shock." If your host country has vast social inequalities and low living standards compared to your home country, you may even feel guilty and depressed when you come back home.

No matter how you experience your return—perhaps you do not notice anything special—it's all a question of re-adapting. And because we humans are very good at re-adapting, reverse culture shock rarely lasts long.

Old Friends

It's never completely accurate to say that nothing at home changed while you were gone. In your community, one of your neighbors may have painted his house, or a shop may have extended its operating hours. In your circle of friends, some relationships may have ended, and a number of your friends may now drive a car or have started university. It is important to respect what your friends have been doing while you were gone. Do not become less interested in their experiences just because you feel that your experiences are so much more important than theirs.

A Thousand Experiences

We humans often feel the need to talk to others about our experiences. But we're also most interested in discussing things that in some way affect us. Therefore, many of your friends may not be interested in hearing about your experience abroad. Of course, many will probably ask you how the year was, but they won't necessarily care to hear all the fine details. This can be frustrating for exchange students, because with so many experiences and impressions, they usually have a lot to tell. But even people who are interested in your story may not understand you very well. It is often said that explaining your year abroad is like explaining a movie to people who haven't seen it. They will hear what you say but they won't really understand it, and often they are not very interested.

In *The Art of Coming Home*, Craig Storti writes, "In the end returnees must accept that those who have not had an overseas experience can never understand things in quite the same way as those who have." Fortunately, there is a group of people who have had experiences similar to yours and who are therefore very easy to talk to: other exchange students, especially those who have been in the same host country. So call them or arrange a meet-up.

It is not uncommon that exchange students become fascinated by their host country, their host family, and their experiences abroad. Students are then often tempted to tell everyone back home how much better everything was in their host country. But be cautious about doing this. Your family and friends can easily feel unappreciated if the only thing they hear from you is how everything was better back in your host country. "Friends and family members sometimes feel rejected and unappreciated if you carry on too much about how wonderful everything was overseas," Storti writes. "If it was so wonderful, they may be thinking, and you liked it so much, then obviously you can't like being back here with them."

Contact with the Host Country

Now it's up to you to maintain the friendships you have made throughout the year. Fortunately, e-mail, Skype, and social media offer an inexpensive way of staying in touch with people from different countries. Services like Facebook make it very easy to see what is going on in other places instantly. It is both time-consuming and unnatural to keep in close contact with everyone all the time. However, you should try to stay in contact with the friends who are most important to you (hopefully this list includes your host family). Send them e-mails and make a phone call once in a while. Contact with friends from your host country is typically more frequent during the first six months after your exchange, and after that it tends to decline. This decline is natural, and you should not worry about it. The people with whom you maintain contact a year or two after you return home are the ones who have potential to be your lifelong friends.

Returning for a Visit

It's always nice to go back for a visit if you have the opportunity to do so. You may want to wait a bit before returning to get the most out of your visit. From one to three years is generally a good time to wait. Perhaps you could also invite your host family or other friends to your home, if possible. They would without a doubt appreciate the opportunity, since you would be giving them a view of your home life, as they gave you a view of theirs.

Chapter 21

Using Your Newfound Knowledge

As a former exchange student, you have acquired special experiences and knowledge. You have gotten to know a new culture, made new friends, and become more independent, and last but not least you have become fluent in a foreign language. All of these qualities can work to your advantage in a variety of situations. In this chapter we will look at how you can take advantage of the knowledge you have acquired during your year abroad.

At School

If you are returning to high school in your home country and your school offers a class in the host country's language, take the class and get some good grades. You may also be able to take an exam that would let you earn course credit without having to attend classes. Talk to your guidance counselor about this as every school is different.

The experience you have gained can help you in other subjects, too, such as history, religion, and social studies. Do not hesitate to impress your teacher with your newfound knowledge. Use everything you have learned abroad to get better grades in school!

International Experience

After a year as an exchange student, you can safely say that you have international experience, and that only gets more and more important in today's globalized society. Many employers value international experience, and you are leaps and bounds ahead of many of your peers in this respect. Therefore, don't forget to include your global experience on your résumé or CV. If you want to go on student exchange while pursuing a university education, or perhaps take a whole degree abroad, your international experience will help you do this.

Languages

If you went to an English-speaking country, you probably speak English fluently by now. Take advantage of that fact! Take a Cambridge ESOL exam or some other language test to get proof of your language skills. Documented English skills will help you in the job market and help you get accepted into a university in the English-speaking world.

If you've learned a language other than English, you also have a huge advantage in the job market. Many employers value candidates who can speak languages other than English. Holiday trips back to your host country will be much more fun now that you know the language!

Maintaining Language Skills

When you have been an exchange student and learned a foreign language fairly well, you never completely forget it. However, many former exchange students feel that they lose their language skills after a while. You may find that it takes a little longer to remember all the words when you have not spoken the language in quite some time. Fortunately, those skills usually come back rather quickly with some practice.

If you learned English, you probably do not have to worry about losing any of your language skills. The next time you go on a holiday abroad, you will probably have the opportunity to speak it quite frequently. If you learned another language, you may have to go back to the host country to speak it again.

One easy way to maintain your language skills is to keep in touch with people you know in your host country. Call them now and then, and send them e-mails in the host country's language. If you do this, you'll keep up your language skills for a very long time.

Chapter 22

Exchange Student Quiz

The correct answers can be found at the end of the quiz.

1. **On your way to your host country, you are having a stopover at a large and unfamiliar airport. All of a sudden you realize that your next flight to your host country has been canceled. What do you do?**

    A) Nothing. You find a comfortable place to sit and wait for someone to call you.

    B) If someone from your exchange organization is present, you speak with him or her. If not, you contact the service desk of your airline and ask how they plan to get you to your host country. You also call your host family or those picking you up at the airport to let them know about the change.

    C) You go online and try to book tickets with another airline.

2. **During school, you leave class to go to the bathroom. When you return, your teacher asks where you have been. When you explain that you went to the bathroom, he yells at you. Apparently, you were supposed to have asked your teacher for permission before leaving the classroom. What do you do?**

    A) You leave the classroom again and head home. It's totally unacceptable to get yelled at for such a small issue.

    B) You yell back that you'll go wherever you want, whenever you want. If the teacher has an issue with that, it's certainly not your problem.

    C) You apologize, explain that you did not know that it was necessary to ask for permission before leaving the classroom, and say it won't happen again.

3. **Your host family has made dinner and you are all sitting around the dinner table. However, the food does not look tasty. What do you do?**

    A) You refuse to eat and then make strange faces every time anyone takes a bite of the food.

    B) You taste a little of the food in order not to be rude.

    C) You use your mobile phone to order some pizza.

4. **You have been in the host country for a week and suddenly feel homesick. What do you do?**

    A) You pack your suitcase and put it in the hallway so that you're ready to go home.

    B) You lock yourself in your room and refuse to talk to anyone.

    C) You talk to your host family, contact person, or others who might be able to help you.

5. **You are at a shopping mall with your friends when you suddenly remember that you had an appointment with your host mother, who is waiting for you at school right now. What do you do?**

    A) You call her to explain the situation.

    B) You do nothing. You will get a ride home with a friend in about two hours, anyway.

    C) You call the school and ask them to explain the situation to your host mother.

6. **For history class, you have been assigned to write five hundred words about the colonial period. You feel that you're not fluent enough in the host country's language to this. What do you do?**

A) You copy the work of a fellow student.
B) You do nothing. There's no point in doing anything when you know you won't be able to write the five hundred words.
C) You explain the situation to your teacher and ask if you can get a smaller assignment or get some extra help with it.

7. **You are an exchange student in a country where everything is cheap, and you have a lot of money compared to others. What do you do?**

A) You show everyone your wealth by using your money to buy as much as possible. When you go shopping, you make sure everyone knows how much money you have spent.
B) You know that big spending can create social distance. Therefore, you are careful not to show off everything you buy.
C) You don't spend much money, but you tell everyone how much money you could have spent if you wanted to.

8. **You are unhappy because you don't have a TV in your room. What do you do?**

A) You get along without it. You can still watch TV with your host family in the living room.
B) You buy a forty-inch flat-screen TV and put it in your room.

C) You call your contact person and demand to change host families.

9. **You realize that the standard of living in your host country is much lower than what you're used to. How do you cope with this?**

    A) You use every opportunity to tell others how simple their way of life is.
    B) You use every opportunity to tell others how much higher the standard of living is where you come from.
    C) You don't do anything. You acknowledge the fact that everything can't be the same as where you come from.

10. **With a month left of your exchange year, you are looking forward to going home. In fact, you have become a little tired of your host country. How do you cope with this?**

    A) If people ask how you feel about going home, you answer honestly and say that you're looking forward to it, but you don't say that you are getting tired of your host country.
    B) You tell your host family and everyone else how tired you've become of your host country.
    C) You call your exchange organization and tell them that their programs last too long and that they should shorten them for all exchange students.

Correct answers for the Exchange Student Quiz

1b, 2c, 3b, 4c, 5a, 6c, 7b, 8a, 9c, 10a

PART
4

EXCHANGE TO THE USA

You step off the school bus and up the steps to the main entrance of your school. On the way to your locker, you greet many familiar faces. The combination to your lock works perfectly, as always. Grabbing only the books you'll need for first period, you head off to homeroom, where the mood is excited, as usual. From your desk you throw yourself into the surrounding discussions about the hot theme of the day: last night's big basketball game with the rival school. Then the bell rings and a familiar voice booms out through the loudspeakers. The whole class stands up, turns toward the American flag, and puts their right hands on their chests. It's time to say the Pledge of Allegiance. By now, you know the pledge by heart and finish off with, " . . . indivisible, with liberty and justice for all." This is followed by the day's announcements. An ordinary school day is about to begin.

Chapter 23

An Introduction to the USA

With an area of over one million square kilometers and a population of more than three hundred million people, the United States is the third largest country in the world. It includes communities of every size, from large, busy cities like New York and Los Angeles to sparsely populated rural areas. It also has extremes of climate, from the hot Texas summers to the harsh Alaskan winters to the year-round warmth of Hawaii. There are long coastlines, impressive mountains, and a number of the world's largest lakes, deserts, and plateaus. There are also enormous forests and spectacular national parks. The USA was described by former president Lyndon B. Johnson as "not merely a nation, but a nation of nations."

Student Exchange to the USA

The USA has a long tradition of hosting exchange students, welcoming more than twenty thousand of them every year! There are many reasons why the USA is such a popular destination for exchange students. The country is big and varied, and its people are very welcoming. In addition, American high schools are known for offering students a wide range of academic subjects, as well as sports and other activities.

CSIET

The Council on Standards for International Educational Travel (CSIET.org) is an American nonprofit organization whose task is to ensure the quality of student exchange programs. The CSIET sets standards for selecting host families, preparing exchange students, and a number of other tasks. Most of the organizations involved with exchange to the USA are listed with CSIET, so if your organization is not, ask why.

History

The USA has a relatively short but nevertheless fascinating history. Although we won't get into the details in this book, we will present a short timeline showing some important events in American history.

Some Important Years in American History

1492	Christopher Columbus discovers America.
1607	The first permanent British colony is established in Jamestown, Virginia.
1620	Some of the first Pilgrims arrive in America on the Mayflower.
July 4, 1776	America's thirteen British colonies join together and declare their independence. The colonies' relationship with England has been strained for a long time and now develops into the conflict known as the Revolutionary War.
1783-84	The colonies win the Revolutionary War.
1789	The USA is born with the enactment of the US Constitution. George Washington is elected as America's first president.
1861	A handful of southern states declare independence from the rest of the USA and secede from the Union. The remaining (northern) states reject their secession, and the Civil War begins. This war costs more than six hundred thousand lives.

1865	The northern states win the war, and the southern states rejoin the Union.
1900s	The USA becomes a superpower as a result of industrialization, economic growth, and victory in the Spanish-American War.
1917-18	The USA fights with the Allies in World War I.
1941-45	The USA fights with the Allies in World War II.
1950-53	The USA is involved in the Korean Conflict.
1969	American astronaut Neil Armstrong becomes the first person to walk on the moon.
1960s-73	The USA fights the Vietnam War.
1990-91	The USA fights the Gulf War, also called Operation Desert Storm.
September 11, 2001 ("9/11")	Terrorists attack the country, including the World Trade Center in New York City and the Pentagon in Washington, DC. Shortly thereafter, the USA declares war on terror and invades Afghanistan.
2003	The USA invades Iraq.
2008	Senator Barack Obama becomes the first African-American to be elected president of the United States.

Government

Like a number of other countries, the USA has divided the powers of government into three branches: executive, legislative, and judicial.

Executive Branch: The President

The president and vice president are elected every four years. The president must have been born in the USA, lived there for fourteen years, and be at least thirty-five years old. The president can be reelected only once and is responsible for a number of tasks. The president is primarily the federal government's chief executive, but he or she is also the commander-in-chief of the military, chief legislator, chief diplomat, ceremonial head of state, and leader of his or her political party.

Legislative Branch: Congress

Congress consists of two chambers: the Senate and the House of Representatives. The Senate is composed of one hundred senators, two from each state. Each senator sits for six years at a time, and a third of the Senate is elected every other year. The House of Representatives consists of 435 members, each of whom sits for a period of two years. The number of representatives delegated for each state is based upon its population.

Judicial Branch: The Supreme Court

The Supreme Court includes a chief justice and eight associate justices. New justices are nominated by the president but must be approved by the Senate. Supreme Court justices have a lifetime appointment unless they are found unfit or become disqualified to serve.

State Government and Federal Government

The USA has a federal structure. This means that the fifty states are self-governed to a certain degree. For example, it is up to each state to pass its own laws, exercise police powers, and determine its own tax rates. However, it is the federal government's responsibility to provide national defense, set international policy, mint money, and tax imports and exports.

Fun fact—Did you know that . . .
in many places in the USA, mail is delivered to your doorstep?

Politics

American politics is dominated by two major political parties: the Democratic Party and the Republican Party. Democrats are viewed as being "liberal" and support a strong government that can ensure the well-being of American citizens through government programs and legislation. Republicans, on the other hand, are viewed as being "conservative." They prefer a small government and business or non-profit solutions to ensure the well-being of American citizens. While political preference and voting habits are considered private matters in many countries, Americans are quite public about the political party they support. During elections, for example, many citizens put up yard signs displaying the name of the politician or political party they support. Prior to elections (whether for mayor, governor, Congress, or president), it's not unusual to get phone calls from enthusiastic supporters who hope they can talk you into voting for their candidate.

The following are some ongoing American political issues that divide the population:

- voluntary abortion (supporters refer to themselves as "pro-choice," opponents as "pro-life")
- the death penalty
- the rights of citizens to own or carry certain weapons
- international involvement and intervention, such as in Iraq and Afghanistan
- stem cell research
- health care

It's important to understand that these are sensitive topics for many people, so you should be a bit cautious if you want to discuss them with people you don't know well.

Geography

The USA shares the North American continent with Canada to the north and Mexico to the south. The Pacific Ocean follows the entire western coastline, while the Atlantic Ocean follows the eastern coastline. Forty-nine American states are located on the mainland, while the fiftieth, Hawaii, lies far out in the Pacific Ocean. People commonly divide the USA into four or more regions: Northeast (New England and mid-Atlantic), South (Southeast and Southwest), Midwest, and West.

The People

Through the years, the USA has welcomed more than seventy million immigrants and still receives between six and eight hundred thousand new immigrants every year. Among its population of more than three hundred million people, 69 percent are white (Caucasian), 12 percent are black

(African-American), 13 percent are Hispanic, 4 percent are Asian, and 1 percent are Native American. Be aware that when Americans talk about race, the terms *Caucasian* and *African-American* are often used instead of *white* and *black*.

A Melting Pot

It's easy to see that the USA is a nation of people from the four corners of the earth. If you chat with an American and tell him or her where you are from, there's a good chance that he or she will also tell you about his or her ethnic heritage, which might include a variety of nations. For example, he or she might be 25 percent Irish, 25 percent German, 25 percent Filipino, 12.5 percent Spanish, and 12.5 percent Polish. Americans are very proud of their multinational heritage and they gladly say "I'm Irish" or "I'm Italian" to express their foreign ancestry and sense of connectedness to others of similar heritage. Many are also eager to stay in touch with far-away relatives from "the old country."

Travel advice
Be careful not to use stereotypes or speak badly about other countries while you are visiting the USA. There's a big risk that you'll offend someone with personal ties to those countries!

Climate

The United States is such a big country that it doesn't have only one climate. Some regions have cold winters and warm summers; others might have either warm or cold weather all year round. The table below shows the average temperatures of some of the largest American cities.

City	Jul-Aug	Jan-Feb	City	Jul-Aug	Jan-Feb
Chicago	24°C (75°F)	-3° C (27°F)	New York	24° C (75°F)	1° C (34°F)
Denver	23°C (73°F)	0° C (32°F)	Orlando	26° C (79°F)	15° C (59°F)
Las Vegas	32°C (90°F)	8° C (46°F)	San Francisco	17° C (63°F)	10° C (50°F)
Los Angeles	21°C (70°F)	13° C (55°F)	Seattle	18° C (64°F)	2° C (36°F)
New Orleans	29°C (84°F)	14° C (57°F)	Washington, DC	25° C (77°F)	3° C (37°F)

"God's Own Country"

On the one hand, Americans are proud of their religious freedom and the separation of religion and state guaranteed by their Constitution, which also forbids public schools from teaching religion. On the other hand, the influence of Christianity is quite obvious in the USA. Many American children begin their school day by saying the Pledge of Allegiance, which includes the phrase *one nation under God*; dollar bills have the motto "In God we trust" printed on them; and when witnesses are sworn into court, they traditionally do so with one hand on the Bible.

Religion is important to many Americans, and it plays a greater role in their lives than it does in many other Western countries. Americans are more often than not quite open and public about their religion. Many go to church every Sunday, and some even attend religious services several times a week. A few Christian groups would seem extremely conservative if viewed through European eyes, while others are more moderate. Many other religions are also practiced in the USA as well, such as Judaism, Mormonism, Islam, and Jehovah's Witnesses to mention some. There is also a growing number of people who are not religious at all, although Christianity still predominates. Exchange students from a number of countries, especially Western ones, may find that religion plays a more important role in the USA than it does in their homeland. Exchange students from other countries may find that religion plays a similar or lesser role than they're used to back home.

As an exchange student, you will not have to adopt the religious beliefs of your host family, but it is important that you respect them and others you meet for their religious choices. Do not criticize others for their points of view.

Travel advice
Never try to convince a believer that God (or another deity) does not exist. You might be thoroughly convinced of it, but you have no stronger proof than he or she has. You will only succeed in offending that person.

"Everything Is Bigger in America"

Not only are cities, cars, and consumer goods bigger in America, but also grocery stores, malls, and shops. In fact, stores like Walmart are so big that they often have a McDonald's built into them.

Pricing

The USA is known for its low prices in comparison with other Western countries. For example, gasoline (petrol) costs about half of what it does in other countries in the West. Brand-name clothing and electronics are also quite cheap, if not the world's cheapest. But be aware that the price you see on the tag is not the price you will end up paying. Price tags in the USA do not include sales taxes. These are added on by the cashier when you pay for your purchase. The tax rate can vary according to product category, and it also varies from state to state. Expect to pay 3 to 10 percent more for your purchases after sales tax is added to the price.

Price examples (2012)	
Product	**US dollars**
Bottled water (0.5 liter)	20¢-$2
Hot dog in a bun	$1.50
Local bus fare	$1
School sweatshirt	$25
Cafeteria lunch	$2-$4

Chapter 24

Living in the USA: Culture and Society

Friendliness

Americans are known for being very sociable and friendly, and it's often easy to start a conversation with an American. Fellow students, neighbors, relatives, teachers, and others will often take the initiative to talk with you and will usually be very friendly. But friendliness must not be confused with friendship.

Just because an American is very friendly to you doesn't necessarily mean that he or she has become your lifelong friend. Suppose that you meet an American and start chatting. After only ten minutes, he or she starts calling you a friend. The conversation gets better and better, and you go on talking for half an hour. But the next time you meet, he or she just says, "Hi," and walks on past. Naturally, you don't quite get it. Many foreign visitors who have had similar experiences later describe Americans as being superficial and fake. But what actually happened in the situation above? This is the most likely explanation: the American probably just thought it was nice to chat with you and was also curious to learn more about you. He or she used the word *friend*, which is a rather vague word in the USA. It is used to describe almost anyone who is friendly toward you. But that's where it ends. Even though you talked for thirty minutes, he or she wasn't yet ready to begin a lifelong friendship. Actually, it takes just as long to form lasting friendships in the USA as it does in any other country.

A Talkative People

Americans love to talk, and silence is often associated with shyness. It's fairly common for Americans to talk to strangers, the people standing in line ahead of them, the person beside them on a plane, and others they meet in their neighborhoods. When you enter into a casual discussion like this, avoid topics like weight, age, and money. Also, it is usually wise to wait until you know the other person very well before talking about religion or politics.

Direct and Indirect Speech

Americans are known for being very straightforward. There might be only one country where people are more direct: Germany. Americans prefer not to speak unclearly or let things go unsaid. We also see this philosophy in American expressions such as "Get to the point" and "Don't beat around the bush" (which means the same thing). If something annoys you, it's expected that you'll bring it up with those involved instead of avoiding the issue and whining about it. This doesn't mean that Americans can't hint about things by making suggestions. However, Americans are generally quite direct.

Politeness

Americans use terms and phrases like *please, thank you,* and *you're welcome* quite often and value politeness in general. If someone opens the door for you or helps you in any way, say thank you. Consider this dialogue between two people:

> Person 1: *sneezes*
> Person 2: "Bless you!"
> Person 1: "Thank you!"
> Person 2: "You're welcome!"

To Americans, politeness says something about your character. It shows others that you don't take it for granted when they do something nice for you.

Modesty and Nudity

Many Western countries have a relaxed attitude about nudity and showing skin. Based on American movies and TV series, one could easily get the impression that the USA is the same way. But reality can be quite different from the movies. The USA is a huge country with vast regional variations in cultural norms. Therefore, you should be careful about being naked or showing too much skin. For example, when you go to or from the shower in your host family's home, you should wear more than just a towel wrapped around your body. Also, you shouldn't walk around your host family's home in just your underwear.

Clothing

Americans tend to wear looser fitting or larger clothes than people in other Western countries, although styles can change. Most Americans would also probably consider it awkward for boys to wear very tight-fitting clothes, although this is not uncommon in many European countries. Also, be aware that for girls, very tight-fitting or revealing clothing (short skirts, low necks, bare waist, etc.) is considered offensive in many parts of the USA. It's not unusual for European exchange students to be approached by officials in their high schools because their clothing is considered unsuitable.

You Are What You Do

Americans are an action-oriented people. The expressions "He's all talk and no action" and "He doesn't walk the talk" are awful judgments to receive in the USA. In conversations with new people, standard questions involve what you do and how you earn your living.

In *Cross-Cultural Dialogues,* Craig Storti says of Americans: "We think of ourselves, to a large extent, as what we do, what we have achieved, and that is how we tend to think of and even judge other people."

If an American doesn't know what you do, how can he know who you are?

Don't be too surprised if you are asked about what you have achieved, what work your parents do, or what you plan to be later on in life. Americans admire people who not only set goals for themselves but also achieve them. Much of the reason money has such high status in the USA is not because it's an indicator of wealth, but because it's a symbol of personal achievement.

This result-oriented (or "the ends justify the means") mentality permeates all aspects of American life. Schools publish the names of the top-ranked students in each graduating class, and the highest-scoring senior, the "valedictorian," is honored with the opportunity to give a speech at the graduation ceremony. High-scoring students are also frequently awarded scholarships from various colleges or the state. Hard work is rewarded in the workplace, as well; many American companies honor certain employees with awards such as Employee of the Month.

There's a Solution to Every Problem

In the USA, the thinking is that there is no problem so great that it can't be solved. Consider, for example, different forms of pollution. The American mentality is that technology will eventually solve these problems. In other words, if you haven't found the solution to a problem yet, it is because you haven't tried hard enough. If one doctor can't cure your medical condition, there's another one who can. Americans like to feel that they are in control. Fate might play some role in their lives, but at the end of the day, Americans feel that they are masters of their own destinies.

Optimism and Trust in the Future

Americans are an optimistic people. They believe the future is full of potential and opportunities for a better life. They consider it important to see the positive side of any situation. Being pessimistic or negative is seen as destructive. In the USA, happiness is one of life's goals. The pursuit of happiness is even mentioned as a human right in the US Declaration of Independence. Americans don't like people to be sad and will try to cheer them up. One way they do this is to offer "comfort food" to friends who are depressed or sad.

Humor

Americans like to be informal and share a laugh with others. People who are humorous can quickly become popular. So if you come out with the right jokes, it's likely that folks will gather around you, expecting you to say something funny. The use of irony is very common among Americans, and it's also important to make fun of yourself sometimes. Americans don't like people who take themselves too seriously, but they love those who joke about themselves.

Laid Back and Informal

Informal and relaxed behavior is generally preferred over formality and stiffness. However, don't confuse informality with bad manners! Being polite is always very important.

Talking in Superlatives

It has often been said that the British express themselves in "understatements," whereas Americans express themselves in "overstatements." Where a Brit would say, "It wasn't bad," a typical American would say, "It was great!" Americans like to present themselves and others in the most positive light. What could come across as bragging in other countries is often simply normal speech in the USA. Americans use superlatives like "the best" and "the finest" much more frequently than do people in other countries. Americans don't consider restraint and humility quite as appealing, as those qualities can sometimes be confused with negativity or shyness. Americans love to give and receive praise. Great, isn't it?

Individualism and Independence

Of all the countries in the world, the USA might be the one with the most faith in the individual. This is well illustrated by expressions like "Where there's a will, there's a way," reflecting the American belief that through hard work, you can achieve anything. One of the first things Americans learn is the importance of self-reliance. Many Americans avoid asking friends and family for help because doing so could make them appear weak or dependent. In many cultures, especially Asian ones, people learn to support a particular group, knowing that group will take care of them if they themselves need help later. In America, another philosophy is more widespread: if everyone takes care of themselves, there will be no problems. Having said that, many Americans donate money to charities or volunteer to help others.

The Land of Opportunity

Americans are proud of the fact that family heritage, social status, and age don't have the same degree of importance in the USA as they do in many other cultures. People are judged by their performance and character. Therefore, you can often climb the ladder of success more quickly in the USA than you can in many other countries. It isn't necessarily the one with most years of experience who is first in line for a job promotion; oftentimes, it's the person who does the best work.

Because people can go from being poor to being rich (from "rags to riches") in the USA, it is often called "the land of opportunity." In the eyes of most Americans, if you work as hard as you can but don't achieve your desired goal, it's only because you didn't work hard enough for it. Many poor Americans do not blame anyone but themselves for the misery they are in.

Time Is Money

The expression "Time is money" is so deeply rooted in American culture that it's hardly said aloud anymore. You do not waste another's time, and you don't ask others to do things for you that you can easily do yourself. For this same reason, efficiency and punctuality are highly valued. If you are going to be more than ten minutes late for an appointment, you should give notice.

Hygiene

Personal hygiene is very important to Americans. They use deodorant, shower, and change shirts and underwear at least once a day. It is important not to smell bad.

Dating and Relationships

American youth commonly start dating at age thirteen, fourteen, or older, depending to some extent on the region where they live and their parents' attitudes. A typical date might involve going bowling, seeing a movie, eating out, or something similar. Parents (or host parents) usually will want to meet the person you're going on a date with before you leave, and it's common practice for the boy to accompany the girl back home to her door by a time specified by her parents. Dating multiple people simultaneously (one on Monday, another on Wednesday) can give you a bad reputation. Spending time with someone of the opposite sex when it is not a date is called "hanging out."

It's worth noting that compared to other Western countries, the USA is generally more conservative when it comes to relationships between guys and girls. In most parts of the USA, it is unacceptable to be alone in your room with someone of the opposite sex. You should stay in common areas when you are with a girlfriend, boyfriend or others of the opposite sex.

American movies and TV series often give the impression that Americans generally have a very open attitude toward sex. But sex is a sensitive issue that many people avoid discussing. In fact, many Americans don't even want schools to teach students about contraception (birth control). It's also worth noting that the typical age for sexual consent in the USA is eighteen, and that there are often severe penalties for someone over eighteen who is arrested for having sex with a minor.

Alcohol and Drugs

The minimum drinking age in the USA is twenty-one, and many people strongly disapprove of alcohol consumption by those under this age. Many Americans also disapprove of alcohol consumption in general. Therefore, as an exchange student to the United States, you should be especially cautious. Your exchange organization will forbid you to drink alcohol as will your host family. So you should really think twice before deciding to drink. Local police often raid parties where minors are reported to be drinking. You don't want your host parents to have to pick you up at the local police station at 2:00 a.m. when they thought you were sleeping over at a friend's house. It's too late for regrets when you're on a plane on your way back home.

Luckily, Americans are good at finding fun things to do without drinking. Staying away from alcohol doesn't mean you have to sit at home alone doing nothing on the weekends!

The use of marijuana, also called "pot" or "weed," is relatively widespread among American youth, and there's a good chance you'll be offered some during your exchange stay. However, it's also important to remember that marijuana is considered a narcotic, and the attitude toward narcotics use is far stricter than it is toward alcohol. If you're caught using marijuana at school, you will be suspended—perhaps permanently. If the police catch you, it's likely that you will lose your residence visa and many host families will demand that you move out. In general, being caught using narcotics is almost always synonymous with getting a one-way ticket for the first flight back home. If you are lucky, you might get away with drinking alcohol, but such mercy is rarely shown to exchange students who use narcotics. Don't take the risk.

Names and Titles

Americans refer to children, friends, and other people they know by using their first name (given name) and to others by using their last name. Don't call a stranger by his or her first name without asking for permission first.

Use the first names of children and others your own age, but always refer to your teachers, your friends' parents, and other adults by using their titles and last names, like "Mrs. O'Boyle" or "Mr. Murray." They will often say something like, "Oh please, call me Katie," after which you should use their first name. However, as a rule you should use only last names when addressing adults.

If the person you are addressing is a doctor or professor, use his or her official title and last name together—"Dr. Hall" or "Professor Stanton," for example. Sports trainers are called "Coach Smith" (for example), or often just "Coach." If you are speaking to a policeman, use the title "Officer": "Excuse me, Officer, I seem to . . ."

Patriotism and Pride: "Proud to Be an American"

Americans are a proud people. They are proud of their Constitution, their standards of democracy and freedom, their rule of law, and their history. Something that symbolizes that pride more than anything is the American flag. It's found in classrooms and on the flagpole at every school, in public buildings, and outside many homes, as well. The flag symbolizes values such as freedom, diversity, and justice—fundamental values upon which the United States was founded.

The national anthem, "The Star-Spangled Banner," is played frequently. Almost all sports events begin with the national anthem, and usually a singer leads the audience by singing it through the loudspeaker system. The correct behavior when hearing the national anthem being played is to take off your hat (if you wear one) and stand with your back straight while facing the flag, possibly with your right hand on your heart. Out of respect, some Americans also close their eyes when singing their national anthem. Another popular patriotic song is Lee Greenwood's "God Bless the USA."

Relationship to Work

Americans work a lot. It's not uncommon for one person to have multiple jobs or to operate small business projects in addition to working a full-time job. Americans often take on additional work to cover expenses like vacations since paid vacations are not a legal right in America.

Travel advice
Read the book *Culture Shock! USA*. It will give you a good overview of the country, and you'll better understand American society.

Chapter 25

The American Host Family

It's a common stereotype that all American families have between two and four children, a dog, and at least one car per family member with a driver's license. But in reality, American families are just as diverse as families anywhere else in the world.

Hosting Regulations

You may find it comforting to learn that hosting exchange students in the USA has become more regulated in recent years. Before a family can host an exchange student, they must be interviewed and provide references. A coordinator will visit their home and take photos of the exchange student's bedroom, bathroom, kitchen, and other areas used by everyone in the family. In addition, a background (criminal record) check will be conducted for every member of the family over the age of eighteen living in the home. This is done to ensure the safety and welfare of all exchange students.

Host Family's Motivation

Why do American families take in foreign exchange students? The answer is complex. Americans are known for their kindness and friendliness toward strangers, and their hospitable nature is a big benefit to exchange students. Americans are also very proud of their own culture and love sharing it with others. Additionally, many Americans dream of traveling to distant lands and by hosting exchange students, they bring a bit of that foreign culture into their living rooms. It's also fairly common for host parents to want to introduce their own children to a different culture through an exchange student.

Housework

Very few American families have a maid, so it's normal for all family members to help out with the housework. Be prepared to spend at least a few hours a week cleaning and doing chores. Try offering help without first being asked. It is a nice thing to do, and your host family will probably be extra nice in return.

Busy Lives and Family Time

Family life in the USA can often be hectic. Many families are busy with young children who need to be driven to and from sports practice, piano lessons, etc. But although many American families struggle with busy schedules, it's also very common for them to gather at least once a day. This can be around the dinner or coffee table, or in front of the TV in the evening. On the weekends, many American families eat breakfast together, sharing pancakes or bacon and eggs. These get-togethers are very important to them.

Curfews and Strict Parents

In America, it is normal for teenagers to have a curfew and for them to tell their parents where and with whom they're going. In any case, it's important to realize that the privileges and responsibilities appropriate for a certain age group in your home country do not necessarily follow you abroad. For some exchange students, this will mean far more personal freedom than they are used to, whereas for others it will mean far less.

Trust

American parents are very concerned about trust. Don't lie to your host parents. Lying is a betrayal of trust, and if you are caught lying it will damage your relationship with them.

Don't Criticize

Criticism won't accomplish anything. It's all right to say that your feelings are hurt or that you think you have misunderstood something, but never let this develop into criticism of your host family's lifestyle.

Hang Out in Common Areas

Unless you're sleeping or doing homework, spending most of your time alone in your room can easily be misinterpreted as a symptom of unhappiness, especially if you keep your door closed. Doing so can easily give the impression that you don't like your host family. Take your book, iPad or laptop computer with you to the living room and sit there, instead. Americans like their family members to stay physically together in the same place.

Tell Them Where You're Going

American host families feel responsible for you and will want to know where you are, what you're doing, and with whom. Tell someone or leave a note when you go out.

Vacations and Holidays

Thanksgiving and Christmas are both holidays when American families get together. Avoid making plans to travel away from your host family during these holidays—it can be misinterpreted as lack of interest in family time.

Use spring break (Easter holiday) to either travel or do things independent of your host family (unless they have made plans to do something with you, in which case you should discuss it with them).

Things to Keep in Mind

Eventually, you will learn your host family's rules and routines. But to help you get started, here is a list of some things to keep in mind:

1. Turn off the lights and/or music when you leave a room unattended (usually your bedroom).
2. Don't bring food or drinks (except water) to private areas of the home, such as your bedroom or bathroom.
3. Clean up after yourself. In general, if you made the mess, clean it up. After you've had a snack or drink, put your dishes in the dishwasher—don't just leave them in the sink.

4. Take off your shoes when you enter the home and put them to one side so other people won't trip over them.
5. Remember to close the kitchen cabinet doors.
6. Observe your host family's mealtime routine. Help out with preparing dinner, setting and clearing the table, washing the dishes, etc.
7. Ask, "How can I help?" Ask this question often so you can find your routine or niche with the family chores. If your family has a dog, maybe you can walk it?

Chapter 26
Preparations and Travel to the USA

Vaccines

Being vaccinated for Hepatitis B is a requirement for all exchange students going to the USA. The vaccine is usually administered in three doses, and the whole process takes about six months to complete. In addition, schools can require you to take or prove that you have taken other vaccines, such as the measles vaccine.

Visa

You'll need a visa to travel as an exchange student to the USA, and all applicants must visit an American Embassy or consulate in their home country to attend an interview and have their fingerprints taken. You should expect to wait a while at the embassy, but the interview itself only takes a few minutes. It is a standardized process conducted over a counter. The interviewer may ask you why you are going to the United States, what you will be doing there, and whether you have a criminal record. After the interview, it usually takes a few weeks to receive your visa by mail.

Fun fact—Did you know that . . .
the USA is the third most visited country in the
world, with well over fifty million tourists yearly?

Medical Check

Exchange students to the USA must undergo a medical
examination before the trip to ensure that they are physically
and mentally healthy.

Cultural and Language Preparations

Exchange students to the USA should read a bit about the
country in advance and get used to using English as often as
possible. Try watching American movies without subtitles or
reading American news online at USAToday.com, NYTimes.
com, or CNN.com.

Luggage

In the past, exchange students could bring two bags weighing
32 kg (70 lb.) on the airplane for free when traveling to the
USA. Nowadays, most airlines have abolished that policy and
let passengers bring only one bag weighing 23 kg (50 lb.) for
free, with the option of paying for additional luggage. But
the rules are changing constantly, so you are advised to check
directly with your airline. Also remember that baggage rules
for domestic flights (those within the continental USA) can be
different from those of international flights to the USA.

> **Travel advice**
> If you like wearing brand-name clothing, don't buy any before you travel to the USA. Brand-name clothing, in particular, is relatively cheap there.

Read more about luggage in chapter 9.

Time Difference

The time in the continental USA is between five and eight hours behind UTC (Universal Coordinated Time).

> **Travel advice**
> Exchange some of your currency into US dollars—about $20-$50—and carry it on your trip. A credit or debit card is not accepted everywhere, and it is good to have cash in case you need it. You can exchange money at the bank before you travel or at any airport.

The Trip

Keep your American host family's address with you on a piece of paper. This is very important, as you may be asked for it during your trip.

Customs Declaration

While on the plane to the USA, you'll need to fill out a customs declaration form. It consists of a number of yes or no questions about what you are bringing along with you. You can bring gifts with you to the USA duty-free up to a total value of $100.

Note: You are not allowed to bring any fruit, vegetables, plants, fresh meat, certain seeds, or other products composed of plant or animal matter into the USA. If you do, you may be fined.

Immigration and Customs

You will have to pass through immigration (for a passport check) and customs (for a luggage clearance) at the first airport you enter in the USA.

You will go through immigration on your way to pick up your luggage. There, you will answer a few questions and have your fingerprints and a photograph taken. Have your passport and visa ready. Afterward, you can get your luggage and proceed through customs. This is also where you will hand in your customs declaration form.

Travel advice
Do you have a long wait until your next plane arrives? Take along an exciting book or create an awesome new playlist on your iPod!

Chapter 27

High School

Yellow buses, your own locker in the hallway, dozens of subjects to choose from, a regular seat in the cafeteria, brief chats around the lockers between classes, school dances and prom, sports practice after school, pep rallies, and the unwritten rule to always attend home games. Going to high school in the USA is not just an education—it's a lifestyle!

School System

The American school system consists of twelve grades. Depending on the grades it encompasses, a school might be categorized as an elementary school, middle school, junior high school, or high school, or a combination of two or more. Below is a chart showing the most common school models:

Grade	Graduation—High School Diploma		Age	Students are called
12			17	Seniors
11	High School		16	Juniors
10		High School	15	Sophomores*
9			14	Freshmen*
8	Junior High School		13	
7			12	
6			11	
5			10	
4			9	
3	Elementary/Primary/Grade School		8	
2			7	
1			6	
K	Kindergarten		4-5	
PK	PreK/Preschool/Nursery School		2-4	

The final three or four years of secondary school in the USA are called "senior high school" (or often just "high school"). Students at these levels are referred to as "freshmen," "sophomores," "juniors," and "seniors" (see figure above). The ninth grade (or freshman year) is considered part of either junior high or high school, depending on the individual school.

*When senior high school is comprised of only three grades, tenth graders are called "freshmen" and ninth graders simply "ninth graders."

Exchange students are placed in grade levels according to their age, English language ability, and academic background. In the USA, people in the same grade often are referred to as "the class of" followed by the year they will finish school (their graduation year). For example, the class of 2020 includes all students who are scheduled to graduate in 2020.

Be aware that the terms *freshman, sophomore, junior,* and *senior* also apply to the first four years of American college (university), and that "the class of 2020" in this instance means the students who will graduate from college in 2020.

Individualized Schedule

High school students have an individualized schedule set up at the beginning of the school year according to their preferences. Although certain core courses are required, students may also pick some electives from a list, and juniors and seniors may often choose from the same elective courses. Because every student has a unique schedule, every class is comprised of a different group of people. Classes are often forty-five minutes long and at many schools the schedule is the same every day, so students have forty-five minutes of each subject each day.

Subjects

Typically, the core classes in high school are English, history, mathematics, and the sciences. In addition to these classes, American high schools are known for offering a broad range of other classes, such as psychology, photography, journalism, speech, drama, Latin, accounting, nutrition, drafting, and marketing.

Travel advice
Choose exciting and unusual subjects.

AP Classes

AP stands for Advanced Placement classes, which are more demanding than ordinary classes (regular classes). Students choose them because they look better on college applications and because they can earn college credit if they score high enough on AP tests at the end of the year. These subjects are more difficult than non-AP versions of the same classes, but you will also learn more by taking them. If you are very interested and motivated, consider choosing one or more AP courses, such as AP psychology or AP chemistry.

Homeroom

Homeroom is a special class, usually held daily, in which students meet with a teacher to receive important announcements. It is similar to a news broadcast of what's going on in the school that day.

Class Participation

American students are expected and encouraged to participate in class discussions. Students who get actively involved are rewarded, and teachers usually strive to make their classes interesting and interactive. Many teachers stress the importance of taking notes, so always bring a notebook and pen to class.

Travel advice
If you don't like taking notes, write down some key words anyway. It may actually help your learning and it will make a good impression on your teacher!

Don't swear or use vulgar language during class time. It is seen as disrespectful, and you may very well receive a detention.

Examinations

Students earn grades based on tests and quizzes (often multiple-choice) and on essays. Short but frequent tests are normal, and unannounced ("pop") quizzes are not unusual, either. Many exchange students find tests in the USA to be easier than the ones at their own school at home, but that doesn't mean that you can pass them without making an effort.

The Student's Role

Your experience as an American student might differ from your experience at home, depending on where you come from. In the USA, you must phone and notify your school if you are going to be absent (not show up). You are not permitted to wander outside of school property during school hours, and if you have to go to the bathroom or get something from your locker, you must get written permission (a "hall pass") from your teacher first. All absences must be justified and arriving late for class or fooling around can result in getting a detention.

Extracurricular Activities

Most schools offer a wide spectrum of after-school and free-time activities. Examples include debate team, chess team, math club, astronomy club, ski club, yearbook staff, school newspaper, school radio, writing club, choir, and band.

Sports and Physical Activities

In the USA, boys' and girls' sports are organized through schools. Each school has its own soccer team, basketball team, cheerleading team, etc. Sports are seasonal (fall, winter, or spring). American football and soccer are typically fall sports, whereas basketball is a winter sport, and baseball is a spring sport. Because of this arrangement, schools are able to offer a variety of sports throughout the year, including American football, soccer, tennis, cross-country running, basketball, volleyball, wrestling, golf, track and field, lacrosse, baseball, softball, and cheerleading.

Tryouts

In order to join a school's sports team, you must demonstrate your potential at a "tryout." Anyone can try out, and the best will be picked for the team.

Within each sport it's also customary to have teams at various levels—see the table below:

Title	Summary
Varsity	This is the first varsity team, generally reserved for seniors and juniors, as well as very talented sophomores.
Junior Varsity (JV)	JV, or "second string," is usually comprised of sophomores and freshmen.
Modified	This team is for students in the first grade of junior high school.

Travel advice
Get involved in sports and other after-school activities; you'll meet new people, and you won't have time to get bored or feel homesick!

High School Spirit

There is something distinctive about going to high school in America. It's not just attending classes from 8:00 a.m. to 3:00 p.m.—it's a social experience. After the last bell, you continue on with sports or clubs, and on weekends it's all about the school dance or the big game, which students attend to support their team. All schools have at least one rival school, and when the two teams meet up for a competition, spirits are very high. Each school has its own colors and mascot. There's a very special feeling among American high school students, which is called "school spirit," and it cannot be explained—it's something that must be experienced.

Recess

With the exception of lunch recess, breaks between classes are usually very brief—sometimes only two or three minutes.

Classrooms

Teachers often have their own classrooms that they decorate with posters and other materials related to the subjects they teach. It is the students, not the teachers, who change classrooms every period. Your desk usually consists of a small writing surface that's integrated into the chair you sit on.

Fun fact—Did you know that . . .
in most states, schools are required to have the American flag visible in every classroom?

Transportation to School

In the USA, schools are responsible for transporting students to school, and most students therefore take the school bus. Those who don't take the bus ride with someone else or drive themselves (in many states in the USA, the legal driving age is sixteen). It's less common to walk or ride a bicycle to school in America, unless you live very close to school.

Fun fact—Did you know that . . .
by federal law, all school buses in the USA must be yellow and be marked with the words *School Bus*?

Lunch

Schools have a daily lunch break that lasts from thirty minutes to one hour. Students eat lunch in the cafeteria or perhaps outside if the school has its own yard. Because between-class breaks are generally very brief, it's less common to eat snacks during those breaks. Almost all schools provide a warm lunch, traditionally served with milk, which can be purchased for $1-$4. You can also bring your own lunch. Americans usually pack their lunch in a brown paper bag. A typical homemade lunch consists of one or two sandwiches, an apple, a small bag of potato chips, and a cookie, some chocolate, or some other small treat.

It's common for students to choose permanent seats in the cafeteria, and the lunch break is used for storytelling, laughter, and planning evening or weekend activities.

School Lockers

Usually students have their own lockers. Prior to the first class, students go to their lockers and put away their things. Between classes, they go back to their lockers and get only the books they need for the next class.

Teacher-Student Relationship

The relationship between students and teachers can be quite formal or very casual, depending on the individual teacher and the school. Moreover, how formal or informal you find the relationship depends on what you are used to at home. Teachers are addressed by their titles and last names (e.g., Mrs. Johnson), and it's important to show respect for them. Talking in class, having a careless attitude, and failing to do homework are looked down upon.

Grading

American high schools use the letters A, B, C, D, and F for grading, with A being the best and D the poorest passing grade. A grade of F indicates failure. Some teachers and schools also report grades in percentages. On a student's official school record, like a report card or grade transcript, the letter grades are converted to numbers (grade points), and a weighted average of these numbers (the grade point average or "GPA") will later be used when the student applies for college.

	Letter Grade	Grade Points	Converted to Percent
	A+		
Excellent	A	4.0	95-100
	A-	3.7	

	B+	3.4	
Good	B	3.0	85-94
	B-	2.7	
	C+	2.4	
Average	C	2.0	75-84
	C-	1.7	
	D+	1.4	
Passing	D	1.0	60-74
Failing	F	0.0	0-59

The Pledge

The Pledge of Allegiance is an expression of loyalty to American values and to the republic of the United States of America. At most schools, it is said daily, weekly, or at least occasionally. When students say the Pledge of Allegiance, they stand facing the American flag, which is found in every classroom, with their right hand over their heart. Here is how it goes:

"I pledge allegiance to the flag of the United States of America, and to the republic for which it stands, one nation under God, indivisible, with liberty and justice for all."

Prom

The annual senior prom is one of the highlights of the year, and there's no holding back on fine clothes. It is often held at an exquisite location, and the two most charismatic or good-looking students are elected king and queen of the prom.

Graduation

This is the closing ceremony marking the end of a student's high school career. It is celebrated with caps and gowns, speeches, and music, and attended by well-dressed parents and siblings. As an exchange student, there's a good chance you might participate in graduation—so that's something to look forward to.

Fun Fact—Did you know that . . .
the use of commas and periods in written numbers in the USA is the opposite of the way those marks are used in many other countries? In the USA, 3,525 = three *thousand* five hundred twenty-five, but 3.525 = three *point* five hundred twenty-five. The comma serves as thousands separator, while the period serves as decimal separator.

Glossary

Word	Definition
A	
absentee	a student who does not show up for class
AP class	the abbreviation for Advanced Placement class—a course that is more difficult and has a more extensive syllabus than other versions of that course
assignment	schoolwork the student has to do at home
assembly	a meeting of the entire student body or a group informational meeting
attendance	when a teacher reads students' names from a list to determine who is present

Word	Definition
C	
cafeteria	a large room where students buy and eat lunch
casual(wear)	a reference to school dress code, meaning that students can dress casually and comfortably (but not sloppily)
cheating	dishonestly improving one's test score (e.g., by copying a fellow student's work)
credits	the number of points that a student can earn by taking a certain subject
curriculum	a plan that shows the combination of subjects required for a given course of education
cut/skip classes	fail to attend a class or classes without notifying the school
D	
detention	a punishment imposed for wrongdoing where the student must stay at school after class hours or on a Saturday
disrupt (a class)	to disturb the lesson
drop out	quit school before one graduates
E	
enrollment	the process of registering a student in school
eraser	a tool used to remove pencil or chalkboard/whiteboard writing. Do not use the word *rubber*, which is a slang term for a condom
essay	a theme-based written work done by a student
F	
faculty	a school's teaching staff
fail/flunk	not pass (finish) a subject or class due to poor performance
formal(wear)	a reference to dress code—elegant clothes for formal occasions
freshman	a ninth grader (a student attending grade 9)

Word	Definition
G	
grade	a class level; also refers to a student's score on classwork
graduation	the ceremony during which students receive their diploma (certificate of completion)
guidance counselor	a faculty member who answers students' questions and offers advice about coursework, college, and careers
H	
hall pass	a written permission slip allowing the student to leave the classroom during class time
homeroom	a designated class period used to provide students with school information and to discuss extracurricular activities with its tutors
homecoming	tradition-filled weekend that takes place every fall when former students return to the school, and which is celebrated with a variety of activities, usually including a parade and a game of American football with a rival school, often followed by a school dance
honor roll	a list of students with high grades—it's considered an honor for a student to be included on this list
J	
janitor	the person who takes care of school maintenance
john	slang for *toilet*
junior	an eleventh grader (a student attending grade 11)
junior varsity	second rank in sports (for younger and less experienced players)
L	
lacrosse	an American team sport
locker	a locked cabinet, usually metal, in which a student stores his or her personal effects such as books
locker room	a room or area designated for changing one's clothes (usually before and after sports)

Word	Definition
N	
nurse	school-based professional who deals with student illnesses, injuries, and other health-related issues
P	
pass	attain an adequate score in a particular subject or course
pep rally	an "assembly" or large gathering of students before a school sporting event intended to generate high spirits among the team and its supporters
period	a block of time used for a class; also refers to a full stop in writing
placement test	a proficiency test used to determine a student's academic level prior to starting a course
principal (vice)	the head of a school (or his/her assistant)
prom	a very formal dance that takes place at the end of the school year
R	
report	to go/ show up as requested somewhere (e.g., "report to the principal's office"); also refers to a research-based written assignment
restroom	toilet
S	
schedule	a weekly plan that shows when and where a student's subject classes will take place
school board	a body (group of people) that governs the school
scholarship	financial aid provided to a student, generally as a reward for academic merit
senior	a twelfth grader (a student attending grade 12)
sophomore	a tenth grader (a student attending grade 10)
spring break	a midterm break in the spring semester (usually during or near the Easter holiday)
student council/ student government	a council comprised of and for students, whose members are elected by the students

Word	Definition
study hall	a period of time without instruction used for homework and private study
substitute (teacher)	a teacher who temporarily replaces another teacher— for example, due to the primary teacher's illness
suspension	a punishment for student misbehavior banning him or her from school for a number of days
syllabus	a list of books and academic articles students will read in a particular subject

T

tardiness	late arrival for class
teacher's pet	a student who is obviously favored by a teacher
track/track and field	a sport that includes foot races and field sports (such as shot put and javelin)
tryouts (or trials)	a test of one's ability and fitness to be a member of a specific sports team

V

valedictorian	the graduating student with the highest grade point average
varsity	a team composed of the best players in a particular sport; also known as "first-string"

Y

yearbook	an annually published book highlighting events in the past school year and including photos of every student in the school

Chapter 28

Practical Information

Time

The USA doesn't use the 24-hour time system but instead the 12-hour system, with the designations AM (ante meridian) and PM (post meridian). As a result, 08:00 is expressed as 8:00 a.m. and 20:00 as 8:00 p.m. See the chart below.

24-hour	a.m./p.m.		24-hour	a.m./p.m.	
00:00	12:00 a.m.	**Midnight**	12:00	12:00 p.m.	**Noon**
01:00	1:00 a.m.		13:00	1:00 p.m.	
02:00	2:00 a.m.		14:00	2:00 p.m.	
03:00	3:00 a.m.		15:00	3:00 p.m.	
04:00	4:00 a.m.		16:00	4:00 p.m.	
05:00	5:00 a.m.		17:00	5:00 p.m.	
06:00	6:00 a.m.		18:00	6:00 p.m.	
07:00	7:00 a.m.		19:00	7:00 p.m.	
08:00	8:00 a.m.		20:00	8:00 p.m.	
09:00	9:00 a.m.		21:00	9:00 p.m.	
10:00	10:00 a.m.		22:00	10:00 p.m.	
11:00	11:00 a.m.		23:00	11:00 p.m.	

Date

In the USA, the month is written before the day. Therefore "8 May 2012" would be written as "May 8, 2012" or, numerically, "05/08/2012." If you write "8 of May 2012" or "8 May, 2012," the date will be understood, but the form will not be considered correct. In any case, you must absolutely avoid writing "08/05/12," as this will be understood as August 5, 2012!

Time Zones

The continental United States is divided into four time zones, and almost all the states also coordinate with Summer Time (known as Daylight Saving Time).

Time Zone	Time in Relation to UTC 19:00	States by Zone
Eastern Time	minus 5 hours = 14:00/2:00 p.m.	From Florida in the south to Michigan/Maine in the north
Central Time	minus 6 hours = 13:00/1:00 p.m.	From Texas/Alabama in the south to North Dakota/Wisconsin in the north
Mountain Time	minus 7 hours = 12:00/12:00 p.m.	From Arizona/New Mexico in the south to Montana in the north
Pacific Time	minus 8 hours = 11.00/11:00 a.m.	From California in the south to Washington in the north

Temperatures

While most of the world now uses the Celsius scale, the USA still measures temperature in Fahrenheit. Note that "body temperature" or 37.8°C = 100°F, and the boiling point for water or 100°C = 212°F.

Celsius	-20°	-15°	-10°	-5°	0°	5°	10°	15°	20°	25°	30°	40°
Fahrenheit	-4°	5°	14°	23°	32°	41°	50°	59°	68°	77°	86°	104°

Conversion from Fahrenheit to Celsius

Standard formula: (°F - 32)/1.8 = °C
For example, a temperature of 60°F would be converted as follows: (60°F - 32)/1.8 = 28/1.8 = 16°C
Quick formula (without a calculator): (°F - 30)/2 = °C

Conversion from Celsius to Fahrenheit

Standard formula: (°C x 1.8) + 32 = °F
For example, a temperature of 100°C would be converted as follows: (100°C x 1.8) + 32 = 180 + 32 = 212°F
Quick formula (without a calculator): (°C x 2) + 30 = °F

Weights and Measures

Americans have their own measures for length, weight, and volume. The US government tried for some time to get Americans to change to the metric system, but it now seems to have given up on that project altogether.

American	Equivalent	Metric	Some uses
Weight			
1 ounce (oz.)		28.35 g	fruit and vegetables
1 pound (lb.)	16 ounces	453.59 g	body weight
1 ton	2,000 pounds	907.19 kg	cars
Volume			
1 fluid ounce		29.57 ml	soda pop
1 pint (pt.)	16 fluid ounces	0.47 l	milk
1 quart	2 pints	0.95 l	milk
1 gallon	4 quarts	3.79 l	gas/fuel
1 barrel	42 gallons	158.97 l (a barrel)	crude oil price
Length			
1 inch (in.)		2.54 cm	body height
1 foot (ft.)	12 inches	30.48 cm	body height, height of mountains
1 yard (yd.)	3 feet	91.44 cm	American football, sports
1 mile (m.)	1,760 yards	1.61 km	highway distance, road signs
Area			
1 square inch		6.45 cm^2	
1 square foot		929.0 cm^2	house size
1 square yard		0.836 m^2	(seldom used)
1 acre	4,840 square yards	4,046.8 m^2	land area measure
1 square mile	640 acres	2.589 km^2	land area measure

Fun fact—Did you know that . . .
a ton in the USA is not 1,000 kg, but 907.2 kg?

Drinking Water

You can safely drink tap water in the USA, although you might find that it tastes different than what you're used to. In many cases, water served in restaurants is tap water.

Currency

The American currency unit is the US dollar, which is divided into one hundred cents.

The symbol for the dollar is $, an *S* with either one or two vertical lines through it. Note that the dollar sign is always placed before the amount; thus it's $40, not 40$.

Americans often use the term *bucks* as a nickname for dollars, so 20 bucks = 20 dollars. Similarly, a *grand* is 1,000 dollars, and so 20 grand = 20,000 dollars.

Coins	
Value	Also Called
1 cent	penny
5 cents	nickel
10 cents	dime
25 cents	quarter
50 cents	half dollar
1 dollar	silver dollar

Bills
Value
1 dollar
2 dollars (rare)
5 dollars
10 dollars
20 dollars
50 dollars
100 dollars

Note that in some situations it can be difficult to pay with bills larger than $20.

Electricity

The USA uses 110/115 volts (not 220 volts, as is typically used in Europe and in many other parts of the world). Therefore, you should check the adapters for the devices you intend to use to ensure they can operate at such a low voltage. Generally, this is not a problem with most chargers for mobile phones and laptop PCs. The plugs used in the USA have two flat metal prongs that you insert into the power outlet, or three metal prongs if the outlet and plug are grounded. Adapters can be purchased at many travel outfitters and airports.

Sending a Package from Home to the USA

It can be a good investment to investigate various alternatives like the official postal service in your homeland, DHL (DHL. com), and United Parcel Service (UPS.com). Often the official postal service will be the cheapest (but usually not the fastest) way to send a package. Investigate the price list to make sure you're getting the best price for what you are sending.

Be aware that you can send gifts to the USA duty-free (so the recipient does not have to pay import duty) as long as their total value doesn't exceed $100 based on the items' cost in American shops.

Tips and Gratuities

In the USA, most services do not include a service charge (tip), and the country has an extensive tipping culture.

In restaurants (but not fast-food restaurants), one should always leave a tip unless the service was very bad! It is normal to tip between 15 and 20 percent. The more satisfied you were with the service, the more you should tip. It is also common to tip other service professionals, such as tour guides and taxi drivers. About 15 percent is a good rule of thumb.

At hotels, it is customary to tip $1-$2 per bag to the porter who carries your luggage to your room, and $1-$5 per night to the maid who cleans your room.

There is only one valid reason for not giving a tip (or for giving a very small tip), and that is if the service was poor or bad. Otherwise, giving a small tip is associated with being miserly. Don't be stingy about giving tips. People who work as waitresses, taxi drivers, etc., usually earn a very low wage and therefore depend on tips to make ends meet.

Annual Events and Important Dates

Description	Date
New Year's Day*	January 1
Martin Luther King Day*	third Monday in January
Presidents' Day*	third Monday in February
Valentine's Day	February 14
St. Patrick's Day**	March 17
Easter (spring break)	March/April
April Fool's Day	April 1
Memorial Day*	last Monday in May
Mother's Day	second Sunday in May
Father's Day	third Sunday in June
Independence day*	July 4
Labor Day*	first Monday in September
Columbus Day*	second Monday in October
Halloween	October 31
Veteran's Day*	November 11
Thanksgiving*	fourth Thursday in November
Christmas Eve	December 24
Christmas Day*	December 25

* public holidays

** celebrated by Irish-Americans with parades and parties

When a holiday falls on a Saturday or Sunday, it is also celebrated on the closest Friday or Monday. Independence Day, Christmas Day, and New Year's Day are exceptions to this rule.

Addresses and Mail

Note that Americans always place the house number before the street name. The city name comes next followed by the state code, a capitalized two-letter combination. After the state code is the postal code (ZIP code). The state name can also be written out in full. For a complete overview of the two-letter state codes, see the State Code List later in this chapter.

Sample mailing address:

Jane Doe
316 Hampton Road
Scranton, PA 15856
USA

Sample mailing address if someone wants to send you something:

Your name
c/o Jane Doe (host parent's name)
316 Hampton Road
Scranton, PA 15856
USA

Note that the postal code is sometimes written using nine numbers (e.g., 15856-2557). The last four numbers refer to a more specific area within the area designated by the first five numbers. The final four numbers are optional.

You can mail a letter from the post office or place it in one of the dark blue mailboxes marked "US Mail." Remember to attach sufficient postage or your letter will be sent back to you!

Transportation

With the exception of its major cities, the USA is sparsely populated, and the best way to get around is to ride with someone who has a car. For travel between major cities, the USA has a well-developed and economical transport system. Most transportation information can be obtained on the Internet, where you can book tickets, as well.

Bus Lines

Greyhound (Greyhound.com): serves the entire USA
Trailways (Trailways.com): similar to Greyhound

Train Line

Amtrak (Amtrak.com)

Major Airlines

American Airlines (AA.com)
Delta Air Lines (Delta.com)
Southwest Airlines (Southwest.com)
United Airlines (United.com)
US Airways (USAirways.com)

Telephone System

American telephone numbers consist of three parts:

Area code + regional code + telephone number: 315-412-3456

The area code is the first three digits (here 315), which are followed by the regional code and finally the number itself. When you call a number within the same area (with the same area code), you don't need to include the area code—for example, you can just dial 412-3456 directly. However, if you call a telephone number with a different area code than yours, you must remember to include the number "1" first (as well as the area code), so the number then becomes 1-315-412-3456.

From a landline, it's usually cheaper to call a number within the same area code (a local call) than it is to call a number outside the area code (a long-distance call).

Toll-free numbers: Numbers in the USA that you can call without being charged are called "toll-free" numbers and begin with 1-800, 1-888, or 1-866.

Emergency number: Dial 911 in an emergency to call the police, an ambulance, or the fire department.

Calling to the USA: Remember the international calling code "+1." Example: +1 315-412-3456.

Calling home from the USA: Remember to use the international call prefix "011," followed by the country code. Example: To call home to (e.g., Germany with country code +49), you might dial 011-49-512-345-67890.

Telephone Cards

Telephone cards or "prepaid phone cards" can be used with most types of phones. They are not plugged in anywhere; instead, you have to punch in a long series of numbers written on the card before you enter the number you are calling. Prepaid cards can be bought in most convenience shops and supermarkets, and they cost $5 and up, depending on how much calling you plan to do.

Mobile Phones

The American mobile network uses GSM 1900. Remember that if you use a mobile phone from your homeland, it's expensive to call home or even to call a local number. It's also extremely expensive for other Americans to call your foreign mobile number, so you should probably get an American phone number.

In the USA, it's very common to buy a mobile telephone together with a calling plan. Such phones are either SIM locked or don't have the option to have SIM cards at all. With the latter, the telephone number is stored inside the phone itself. Mobile phones are usually permanently locked to the network system, and if you want to change to a different network, you must buy a new phone. On the other hand, mobile phones in the USA are quite cheap, starting at about $20, including a prepaid card.

Therefore, there are two ways to get an American mobile phone number. The first is to buy an American SIM card. At least two providers, AT&T and T-Mobile, offer one for about $10. Remember to ensure that your mobile is not locked to your home provider. With your SIM card you will get a certain amount of credit, which you can refill later. The second method is to buy a new mobile with a built-in number. You can also buy a new mobile including a SIM card from T-Mobile or AT&T.

You are strongly advised to check and compare plans from at least two providers. As you will be staying in the USA for a long time, you can save a considerable amount of money by choosing the best plan.

Note: In the USA, you also pay to receive both SMS and phone calls.

Major Mobile Telephone Providers

AT&T (ATT.com)
Sprint Nextel (Sprint.com)
T-Mobile (TMobile.com)
Verizon (Verizon.com)

States Code List

State	Code	Also Called	State Capital
Alabama	AL	The Heart of Dixie	Montgomery
Alaska	AK	Last Frontier	Juneau
Arizona	AZ	Grand Canyon State	Phoenix
Arkansas	AR	Natural State	Little Rock
California	CA	Golden State	Sacramento
Colorado	CO	Centennial State	Denver
Connecticut	CT	Constitution State	Hartford
Delaware	DE	First State	Dover
District of Columbia*	DC		Washington
Florida	FL	Sunshine State	Tallahassee
Georgia	GA	Peach State	Atlanta
Hawaii	HI	Aloha State	Honolulu
Idaho	ID	Gem State	Boise
Illinois	IL	Prairie State	Springfield
Indiana	IN	Hoosier State	Indianapolis
Iowa	IA	Hawkeye State	Des Moines
Kansas	KS	Sunflower State	Topeka
Kentucky	KY	Bluegrass State	Frankfort
Louisiana	LA	Pelican State	Baton Rouge
Maine	ME	Vacationland	Augusta
Maryland	MD	Free State	Annapolis
Massachusetts	MA	Bay State	Boston

State	Code	Also Called	State Capital
Michigan	MI	Wolverine State	Lansing
Minnesota	MN	North Star State	St. Paul
Mississippi	MS	Magnolia State	Jackson
Missouri	MO	Show Me State	Jefferson City
Montana	MT	Treasure State	Helena
Nebraska	NE	Cornhusker State	Lincoln
Nevada	NV	Silver State	Carson City
New Hampshire	NH	Granite State	Concord
New Jersey	NJ	Garden State	Trenton
New Mexico	NM	Land of Enchantment	Santa Fe
New York	NY	Empire State	Albany
North Carolina	NC	Tar Heel State	Raleigh
North Dakota	ND	Peace Garden State	Bismarck
Ohio	OH	Buckeye State	Columbus
Oklahoma	OK	Sooner State	Oklahoma City
Oregon	OR	Beaver State	Salem
Pennsylvania	PA	The Keystone State	Harrisburg
Rhode Island	RI	The Ocean State	Providence
South Carolina	SC	Palmetto State	Columbia
South Dakota	SD	Mt. Rushmore State	Pierre
Tennessee	TN	Volunteer State	Nashville
Texas	TX	Lone Star State	Austin
Utah	UT	Beehive State	Salt Lake City
Vermont	VT	Green Mountain State	Montpelier
Virginia	VA	Old Dominion State	Richmond
Washington	WA	Evergreen State	Olympia
West Virginia	WV	Mountain State	Charleston
Wisconsin	WI	Badger State	Madison
Wyoming	WY	Equality State	Cheyenne

*Federal district

American English vs. British English

There aren't many differences between American English and British English, but there are some. Even though Americans will understand what you mean with words like *bank note*, *sweets*, and *cinema*, you will rarely hear Americans use them. Instead, they will say *bill*, *candy*, and *movie theater*. There are also spelling differences, and at school you could discover red marks underneath words if you've spelled them using British English.

The differences between the two types of English generally can be divided into three groups: spelling, expressions, and words.

Every nonnative English speaker who goes to the USA should consistently use American English. You will probably add a number of American expressions to your vocabulary without even realizing it anyway, and if you try to stick to British English, you will end up speaking "Ameritish English" (a mix).

Spelling Differences

Certain groups of words are spelled differently in American English than they are in British English. For example, the British vowel combination *ou* often becomes simply *o* in the USA, and in certain words Americans use *z* instead of the British *s* and the ending *er* instead of the British *re*.

British English	→	American English
harbour, colour, neighbour, odour	→	harbor, color, neighbor, odor
organise, recognise, realise	→	organize, recognize, realize
centre, theatre, metre, litre	→	center, theater, meter, liter

Expressions

Different uses of prepositions, verbs, and other parts of speech are among the ways American English is distinguished from British English. Here are two examples:

British English	→	American English
at school	→	in school
get your picture taken	→	have your picture taken

Words

Here are some vocabulary differences between American English and British English:

British English	American English
flat	apartment
entrée, starter	appetizer
cash machine	ATM
toilet	bathroom/restroom
bank note	bill
thousand million	billion
sweets	candy
crisps	chips
biscuit	cookie
primary school	elementary school
lift	elevator
rubber	eraser
Christian name	first name
American football	football
chips	French fries
petrol	gas
surname	last name
queue	line
angry	mad
film	movie

cinema	movies/movie theater
serviette	napkin
trousers	pants
public school	private school
return ticket	round-trip ticket
football	soccer
jumper	sweater
lorry	truck
holiday	vacation

Acknowledgments

Many talented people have contributed to this book, and I am grateful to each and every one of them.

First and foremost, I would like to thank the many exchange students whose comments and feedback have made this a much better book, especially Ben G. Craven, Elisabeth Gåthe, Felix Kopka, Henrikke Bryn, Iris Rekola, Kaja Marie Brodtkorb, Matheus Luiz Puppe Magalhães, Monica Cristina Poujol Fabara, and Niina Väyrynen.

I would also like to express my deep appreciation to the experienced exchange organization staff and coordinators, Anja Bekens, Inga Menke, Katie Gang, Marcel Aßmann, and Uli Selbach, for their insightful and valuable comments.

Heartfelt thanks go to Martin Brennan, the former director of the International House at UC Berkeley, for his help with the intercultural content of this book.

Special appreciation also goes to my competent cover designer Jacob Holmberg; to my creative illustrators Lars Petter Hermansen and Ola Olsen Lysgaard; to my talented American friends Matt Allison, Jack O'Brien, David Gilliam, and Daniel Stratton for helping improve the language in the book; and to everyone else whose contribution, small or large, helped me along the way.

Bibliography

AFS Intercultural Programs. *The AFS Story*. 2nd ed. Switzerland: JPM Publications, 1997.

Bachner, David, and Ulrich Zeutschel. *Students of Four Decades*. Münster: Waxmann, 2009.

Carnegie, Dale. *How to Win Friends and Influence People*. United Kingdom: Vermilion/Ebury Publishing, 2006.

"CSIET Standards for Long-Term International Educational Travel Programs," 2006, www.csiet.org.

De Jongh, Floor. *Teenage Explorers*. Oslo: KREBS Forlag, 1999.

Hammer, Mitchell R. *Assessment of the Impact of the AFS Study Abroad Experience*. New York: AFS Intercultural Programs, 2005.

Hansel, Bettina. *The Exchange Student Survival Kit*. 2nd ed. Boston: Intercultural Press, 2007.

King, Nancy, and Ken Huff. *Host Family Survival Kit: A Guide for American Host Families*. 2nd ed. Yarmouth: Intercultural Press, 1997.

Ledru, Raymond, and John Chandler. *Manuel de Civilization Américaine*. 2nd ed. Paris: Ler Cycle Universitaire, 2000.

Nisbett, Richard. *The Geography of Thought*. Boston: Nicholas Brealey Publishing, 2003.

"Preventing and Treating Homesickness," by Christopher A. Thurber and Edward Walton, 2007, www.aappublications.org.

Rauner, Max. *Als Gastschüler in den USA*. Germany: Reise Know-How Verlag Grundmann, 2006.

Storti, Craig. *Cross-Cultural Dialogues: 74 Brief Encounters with Cultural Difference*. Boston: Intercultural Press, 1994.

Storti, Craig. *The Art of Coming Home*. Yarmouth: Intercultural Press, 2001.

Storti, Craig. *The Art of Crossing Cultures*. Yarmouth: Intercultural Press, 2001.Wanning, Esther. *Culture Shock! USA*. New York: Graphic Arts Center Publishing Company, 2006.